D0407032

A Testament of Faith

A Testament of
FAITH

by

G. BROMLEY OXNAM

SAN DIEGO PUBLIC LIBRARY

Little, Brown and Company • BOSTON • TORONTO

COPYRIGHT, ©, 1958, BY G. BROMLEY OXNAM

ALL RIGHTS RESERVED. NO PART OF THIS BOOK MAY BE REPRO-
DUCED IN ANY FORM WITHOUT PERMISSION IN WRITING FROM THE
PUBLISHER, EXCEPT BY A REVIEWER WHO MAY QUOTE BRIEF PAS-
SAGES IN A REVIEW TO BE PRINTED IN A MAGAZINE OR NEWSPAPER.

LIBRARY OF CONGRESS CATALOG CARD NO. 58–6027

FIRST EDITION

The author wishes to thank the following for permission to use
material published by them: Maxwell Anderson, for passages from
Key Largo; the Macmillan Company, for quotations from *Collected
Poems* by Vachel Lindsay (1925) and *Poems* by John Masefield
(1953); the Muhlenberg Press, for excerpts from *The Valley of the
Shadow* by Hanns Lilje (1950); and Doubleday & Company, Inc.,
for the excerpt from *How to Believe* by Ralph W. Sockman (1953).

*Published simultaneously in Canada
by Little, Brown & Company (Canada) Limited*

PRINTED IN THE UNITED STATES OF AMERICA

OCT 16 '58

To
"Ruthie" and "Wobbie"
or, more formally, to
Ruth McCormack
and
Robert McCormack
with a grandfather's love

Introduction

WHEN I was invited to do a book on my faith, I assented readily. I had declared the Christian faith for many years and had sought to witness to the faith in both word and deed. I thought I had undertaken a simple task. I was wrong. It has been very difficult. Perhaps my respect for the convictions of others has kept me from dogmatic proclamation and has left me without an easily phrased summary of faith which can be presented with a "take it or leave it" spirit. Then, too, there is much in the differing formulations of the faith that I cannot in honesty reconcile with what I believe to be the character of God and the mind of Christ.

I have often wondered what Jesus would think and do if He were to sit in some church councils or ecumenical assemblies in which the major churches of the world meet to consider such questions as faith and order, life and work. Our Lord told simple stories. They were full of light and drove the dark away. Like the morning sun they brought color to nearby flowers and trees and defini-

tion to mountain masses far away. He taught as one having authority. He spoke as never man had spoken. "A
new commandment give I unto you that ye love one another even as I have loved you." In these eighteen words
are fourteen words of one syllable, two of two syllables,
and two of three syllables. His speech lacks technical
jargon and theological fiddle-faddle. His stories were
brief and free from philosophical verbiage. "He that
hath seen me hath seen the Father." What would He
have done with the speculative fustian present in writers
who consider the Trinity? I doubt not that many of the
learned would dismiss His teaching as lacking profundity.
But the common people heard Him gladly. I can understand the Beatitudes, the stories of the Good Samaritan
and the Prodigal Son, and it is clear what He had in
mind when He denounced the scribes and Pharisees as
hypocrites.

I find it hard to understand men who "accept Christ"
and then become sadistic as they deal with others who try
to "love God with heart and mind and soul, and brother
as self," but who cannot in honesty accept the obscur-
antism that is presented as "the faith," especially when
the presentation is accompanied by the clanking of In-
quisition chains and the crackling of the fires at the stake.
The coercion by the bigoted is in itself a rejection of the
spirit of Christ. He relied upon the compulsion of love.
If I were called upon to choose one word to describe
Christianity, it would be love. I believe God is love. I believe nothing can separate me from the love of God. I
believe God was in Christ reconciling the world unto

Himself. I believe God sent Jesus because He "loved the world."

So I have written about God, Christ, and immortality, and what I have written is grounded in the fact of God's love. I have considered prayer and the forgiveness of sin, and have set down a few words about the Church. Here again, I move out from the love of the Eternal and the love manifest in His Son. I have dared to say I believe in man at a moment when many discount man in the name of a religion that exalts him. I believe in man because he knows the meaning of love, a love that transforms and never disappears. It is in love that our redemption lies.

If these words prove helpful, I shall be happy. If they occasion much debate or develop doubt, I shall regret it. They are but the expression of one man who has tried to love God. I know so little about God, but what I know I have seen in the face of Jesus, and that is enough for the journey. When at last I know as I am known, I believe *that* knowledge will validate my conviction that God is love.

G. Bromley Oxnam

Washington, D.C.

Contents

A Testament of Faith

CHAPTER I

I Believe in God

I HAVE REPEATED the opening affirmation of the Apostles' Creed since boyhood. "I believe in God, the Father Almighty!" One of my earliest recollections is that of hearing my father pray:

> O God, our help in ages past,
> Our hope for years to come,
> Our shelter from the stormy blast,
> And our eternal home!

My mother read the great stories of the Great Book to us each night before we went to sleep. I was reared in the Christian tradition, and thought that everybody believed there was a God. There were times when I was confused. It was hard to understand how a God who loved everybody could be so cruel. Killing the first-born of the Egyptians did not seem fair to me.

Nonetheless, I was at church every Sunday and finally became a member. And as the Sundays came and went, again and again I declared, "I believe in God, the Father Almighty." It was like the Pledge of Allegiance that I learned at school, and repeated with appropriate gesture: "I pledge allegiance to the flag of the United States of America and to the republic for which it stands."

I inherited my faith and my freedom. Many millions today are reared in a society in which faith in God is looked upon as superstition, and in which freedom is a word used by tyrants who regiment the individual and exploit his mind by coercing him into conformity. "When I was a child, I thought like a child, I talked like a child, I argued like a child; now that I am a man I am done with childish ways." That was true for the Apostle Paul, but it is not true for most of us. Too many of us carry immature conceptions of religion into adult life. I fear I am one of them.

I have met many theologians and have listened to their lectures with respectful attention. I have labored through their heavy volumes. I must admit regretfully that I still see through a glass darkly. Their discussions in ecumenical conferences confuse me. I know I must be at fault. These are learned men. I am sure that theology involves technical jargon just as physics, biology, and chemistry do. Theologians deal with ultimate questions. There are no easy answers.

Can an intellectually honest man believe in God? Is it really true that the Eternal who notes the sparrow's fall cares for me? Is it a fact that God's love for man is not an impersonal love for mankind in general but a personal love for me in particular? Is there an Eternal One? Or have we created God in our own image, just to satisfy some imaginary need?

I have trudged the weary road of doubt. I, like you, have wondered. If there be a Supreme Being, why should he be so interested in a bit of life, existing for a few years, upon a tiny planet — hardly discernible in the vastness of the universe? I, like the Psalmist, have said:

> When I consider Thy heavens, the work of Thy
>   hands . . .
> What is man, that Thou art mindful of him?

Is there an answer here that satisfies?

Frankly, I repeat the words "I believe in God, the Father Almighty" with complete assurance. I believe this is my Father's world. I believe moral law is written into the nature of things. I believe God is a God of love and of justice. Bishop Robert E. Jones, the distinguished Negro leader, once said, "Whenever I hear anybody knockin' God, I just say, 'Good-by, hammer.'" Upon what do I base this faith? I must be honest with you. I am not a theologian. Nor am I a physicist. I would be a fool to discount the physicist. Many fools ridicule the theologian. But deep and consistent thought is surely as essential in theology as in physics.

Some time ago I was invited to deliver a lecture in the Great Issues course at Dartmouth College. There was but one requirement. I must deal with religion. The lecture is given to the entire student body, and the lecturer remains for a second day to answer any question put to him by members of the senior class. The first question went to the root of the matter. A senior said, "I liked your definition of God; it was satisfying. My question is this: Is there any reality that corresponds to the definition?" I longed for the presence of one of my friends, Reinhold Niebuhr or Walter M. Horton or Robert Calhoun. They are competent theologians and would have replied in terms satisfying to the intellectual. I know that answers must be given. Christianity is challenged today by a dynamic and determined atheism that strikes at the foundations of the faith.

Thirty-one years ago, I was a member of a delegation that visited Russia. The revolution had occurred but nine years before. The civil war followed. Millions had been killed. The Bolsheviki were in power. Lenin was dead but thousands stood in line to enter the mausoleum and to look upon his face. Religion was under attack. Church leaders were in hiding or in prison. We met perhaps forty of the leaders of the regime. Two thirds of the forty were later purged, but at that time they were masters — such persons as Kamenev, Zinovieff, Tomsky, Trotsky.

At the close of our study we were asked to give our impressions of what we had seen. It fell to me to recount what we had seen in the field of religion. I spoke frankly and critically, and condemned dogmatic atheism as unscientific. Lunacharsky, then the head of education in Soviet Russia, rose and said, "I cannot understand you. I am informed that you are a man of the schools. How can any man trained in a university hold to such superstition? We shall not attack religion in the future. We will not have to. We shall train our youth in the scientific method and ground them in a philosophy of materialism. Religion will die. It cannot survive the light of truth. And your religion above all the rest! It is designed to keep people in subjection. You speak of meekness, and of love, of the second mile. This is for the exploiter's use. It is a tool to be used by tyrants to maintain class privilege." More than thirty years have passed. Religion is not dead, not even in Russia. But atheism as a philosophy has been extended and today millions who are under Communist domination are reared in schools where theism is repudiated.

Atheism is not confined to the Communist. There is a practical atheism present in our own society. Many repeat, "I believe in God, the Father Almighty," but they insist that God is not relevant to the political, the social, the economic life. They hold that "to the strong belong the spoils." They say, "Self-interest is the only sufficient motive to drive men to production." They argue that "moral right must bow to economic necessity." They reject the Christian doctrine that a man's talents, power, and property are held in trust, to be administered in accord with God's will. They embezzle power. Preachers are told to mind their own business and to preach the simple gospel.

Confronted by a world-wide movement that rejects the idea of God as superstition or as the cleverly contrived conception of a ruling class to be used to keep the masses in subjection, and confronted by influential persons and movements that affirm faith in God but in fact repudiate the faith by insisting God is not relevant to daily life, it is clear that the affirmation with which the Creed begins is under attack.

The attackers must be attacked. Men and women who believe in God refuse to be placed upon the defensive.

I believe in God. It is not easy for me to tell why I hold this faith. I am sure I cannot give scientific proof and thereby demonstrate the fact of God.

I turn to Jesus and do not find "proof," nor do I find involved theological argument. He began His ministry by assuming the fact of God and by announcing that God had anointed Him to preach the gospel to the poor. The sermon was not well received. The congregation ran Him out of town. In the Sermon on the Mount, He tells us the pure in heart shall see God; He speaks of God's throne; teaches His followers to pray; addresses God as a Father; insists we cannot serve God and mammon; points out that God cares for the lilies; and calls upon men to do the will of the Father who is in heaven. In a word, Jesus takes God for granted. He tells simple stories that even a child can understand — the Prodigal Son, the Good Samaritan, and many more — but does not think it necessary to turn to the heavy and at times obscure terminology of the theologian.

As I have said, I am not a theologian. That will soon be evident. I know that faith must be undergirded with reason, and I doubt not that the theologian occupies a

key place in a day when there is a world-wide struggle
for the minds of men. But for me, I must set down a
simple story to explain why "I believe in God, the Father
Almighty."

I was raised in a Christian home. My father and
mother were devout Christians. Grace was said at meals;
the day was begun with family prayer; and Sunday was
a day of worship and of rest. Each evening Mother read
to us for an hour. Biblical stories were a prominent part
of the bedtime reading. There was no radio, no motion
picture, no television. On Sunday we went to Sunday
School and attended the morning service of worship. In
the afternoon, Mother read to us, and as we listened,
we cut out pictures, painted with water colors, or lay
on the fur rugs that bore testimony to my father's hunt-
ing. A taxidermist had done a splendid job with a great
cinnamon bear, and each one of us wanted to lie on
the bear rug, so that its great head, with the big glass
eyes, might be a pillow. I must have been twelve or
thirteen before I was allowed to ride a bicycle on Sunday afternoons after reading. Mother read extraordinarily well, and the Sunday afternoon was an event
as well as an education. In it all, God was as much
a part of our thought as sunshine or rain, flowers or
trees. We "said" our prayers at Mother's knee. But there
were questions and I recall a sense of resentment when
Mother read the stories that appeared to make God do
unfair things.

My first queries as I now recall them dealt more with
the character of God than the existence of God. Whether

atheists existed in the foxholes of World War II, I do not
know, but there was no atheism in our home. God was,
and that was all there was to it. Perhaps a boy raised in
the atmosphere of a Communist home may grow up an
atheist without thinking much about God's existence. I
don't know. I know I grew up believing in God.

The fact that I was taught to pray convinced me that
God knew me as an individual. I am not sure that I was
fully aware of God's love. I knew He was not a policeman. We did not have friendly traffic policemen in those
days. A "cop" was a blue-coated fellow with a domelike
hat and a big club who was called in to enforce law, or
take boys off to jail. No, God was not a "cop," but He
was not really like a father. There was an element of
fear present in our approach. He had punished so many,
and we had learned that He was a "jealous" God. He
punished even to the third and fourth generations, whatever that meant.

But we did learn that He pitied His people. He was
like the shadow of a rock in a weary land. Father once
told me how cool it was in the shadow of a great rock
when the sun blazed upon the desert. Saying prayers
was more like telling beads, something to be done; almost something that got me in right with the powers
that be. I doubted. I remember that vividly. Not
that I doubted God! But that God could do some of
the things He was reported to have done! In our home,
the Scriptures were the inspired word of God, and the
Old Testament stories were a record of what God had
actually done. It was hard for a boy to understand how

God could be a God of love and still could slay little children.

All of this was a boy's approach to a fundamental proposition. God must be a morally obligated Being. God must be righteous. Assuming there is a Supreme Being, the question of His character is fundamental. How could He lead us in paths of righteousness if He Himself were not righteous? My father had a strong sense of justice, and I have a vague recollection of an explanation that did not explain when I asked him about the first-born of the Egyptians who were slain.

Strangely enough, this question carried over through the years, and when I was invited to give the famous Lyman Beecher Lectures at Yale University, it expressed itself in an illustration that has been bandied about the world. I wanted to stress the fact of the righteousness of God. The lectures were upon the theme "Preaching in a Revolutionary Age." It had seemed to me that in a revolutionary period it was essential to lay hold upon ethical absolutes. There must be some things that are eternally true. One of these absolutes, at least it seemed so to me, was that God is good, that He is holy, that He is righteous. He, the Creator, cannot by His very nature do wrong.

In the reading that preceded the writing of the lectures, I ran across a few paragraphs from Hugh Walpole. They appear in his novel *Wintersmoon*. I wrote, "Hugh Walpole, in *Wintersmoon,* tells of a father and son at church. The aged rector read from the Old Testament, and the boy learned of the terrible God who sent plagues upon the people and created fiery serpents to assault them. That night when the father passed the boy's bedroom, the boy called him, put his arms around his father's neck, and drawing him close, said, 'Father, you hate Jehovah. So do I. I loathe him, dirty bully!' " I went on to say, "We have long since rejected a conception of reconciliation associated historically with an idea of a Deity that is loathsome. God, for us, cannot be thought of as an angry, awful, avenging Being who because of Adam's sin must have his Shylockian pound of flesh. No wonder the honest boy in justifiable repugnance could say, 'Dirty bully.' "

I tried to point out that injustice is an offense, and inequality a stench, in the nostrils of Jehovah also. Such must be denounced by preachers in a revolutionary age; and, just as our thought of God had to be moralized to represent him to moral men, so too our conception of God's world must be made moral if man is to say in honesty, I believe in God, the Father Almighty, Maker of heaven and earth. The purpose was to make it clear that the God whom we worship, the God revealed in Jesus Christ, is a righteous Being.

To my utter amazement, I found that I was being quoted by some of the fundamentalist periodicals as having said God is a "dirty bully." I did not know at that time that the story was being spread deliberately by a man who had been unfrocked by his own church for violation of his ordination vows and who appeared to be spending the rest of his life in striking back by misrepresenting the leaders of the great churches and in attacking such significant Christian agencies as the World Council of Churches and the National Council of Churches; and with utter disregard of the Biblical injunction "Thou shalt not bear false witness" was sending this bit of misrepresentation to the far corners of the earth. Dr. W. A. Visser 't Hooft, the distinguished general secretary of the World Council of Churches, said he was asked when in Africa, "Is it true that one of the presidents of the World Council of Churches believes that God is a 'dirty bully'?" Picked up by little men who forget that we are to "judge not," who seem to forget that at the heart of the Christian religion are truth and love, the libel has been printed and reprinted, and I have found it in the Orient and in Latin America, in the South Pacific and in Europe. I mention it here, not to answer these gentlemen — they are not interested in the truth — but to deal with a fundamental question, one that for me antecedes the basic question of existence, namely, the issue of character. I could not worship an unrighteous being.

Recently in Singapore a distinguished Chinese physician of considerable wealth, a leader in the Christian community, raised this question. I said, "Doctor, you are a man scientifically trained and I think will be the first to appreciate a very brief answer. The Bible records the age-long search of man for God, and God's never-ending quest for man. The Bible is an honest book. It records with fidelity the limited notions of God held by men in primitive days.

"In the beginning, some men thought of God as a tribal deity. He was their God, who when properly propitiated would strike down their enemies. There were other gods and sometimes after defeat the people would turn to false deities who had demonstrated their power in battle. The Bible records all this. A person who is still caught in the toils of a false understanding of the Bible will be unable to extricate himself. But a person who has discovered one of the key words in the interpretation of the Bible is soon freed. That word is 'development.' There was development in man's understanding of God. The Bible faithfully records the moralization of the conception of God.

"It was Amos, the prophet of the eighth century, who made it plain that God is righteous. Amos lived in a day when riches were pouring into his country, but the poor were becoming poorer and the rich richer. This lonely herdsman thought deeply. The Eternal had found a mind and a heart capable of understanding, and a voice able to speak. Amos could not believe that transgressions by the chosen people were any less transgressions than those of foreigners. A lie is a lie whether told by a Communist or a fundamentalist. Amos reached the conclusion that God will not withhold His punishment from the chosen people if they do wrong any more than from the enemy. An unjust people will reap the whirlwinds of rebellion, whether Jew or Gentile. He goes to a great feast at Bethel and calls out to the assembled leaders, 'Thus saith the Lord; For three transgressions of Damascus, and for four, I will not turn away the punishment thereof.' The crowd is delighted. Damascus was an enemy state. He mentions other similar states. And then when he has that audience in his grasp, he cries, 'Thus saith the Lord; For three transgressions of Israel, and for four, I will not turn away the punishment thereof; because they sold the righteous for silver, and the poor for a pair of shoes.' In the teachings of the prophet Amos, the Bible makes it abundantly clear that God is righteous.

"Hosea saw God as a Being of love. Isaiah insisted He was a universal Being. Ezekiel called for personal piety, and so on through the centuries the conception of the Eternal moved closer and closer to the reality which the Eternal is. Finally, God was revealed in a Person, 'Jesus Christ, His only Son our Lord,' as the Creed puts it."

I then asked the doctor, "Does any intelligent and honest Christian really believe that God as revealed in Jesus, who Himself could tell us that it was better that a millstone were hanged about a man's neck than to offend little children, does anyone believe that such a God would have slain the innocent first-born of the Egyptians because Pharaoh's heart had been hardened by God Himself? Herod might have done such a ghastly thing. Hitler might, but God? Never! The Bible is trustworthy. It is validated by its honesty. What is recorded there is the honest record of what men then thought about God."

I said, "Doctor, I would not commit so terrible a crime. You would not. Would Jesus? It is almost irreverent to ask the question. To say that one affirms God is a 'dirty bully' when he quotes a boy's repugnance in the presence of a primitive and tribal thought of God is to blaspheme. I used the illustration for the precise purpose of stressing the morality of God. By His very nature, He cannot be a bully. He is limited by His nature. A god of truth cannot lie, a god of goodness cannot do an evil thing. A god of justice cannot be unjust, nor can a god of love do an unlovely thing."

The doctor looked at me for a moment and said, "Bishop, I understand you fully. What you mean is this: If a man says an individual is ugly when he is handsome, the fact that he says it does not make the handsome man ugly."

I replied, "Doctor, that is precisely it. God is what He is, what He has always been, however limited man's notion of the Eternal may be. The Bible in its honesty records these limited notions and the long, long development of man's understanding until at last, in Jesus Himself, the Word becomes flesh, we behold the Eternal as He is."

For me, at least, I have to start with the goodness of God, the righteousness of God. He must be One upon whom we can count, the same yesterday, today, and forever, not only that the sun will rise tomorrow, that the laws at work in the physical universe are not to be abrogated by caprice, but that no favorites are to be played. If I deliberately jump off a building, the law of gravity is going to operate no matter how many prayers I may offer on the way down.

God for me is more than impersonal goodness. I have been assuming intelligence, infinite intelligence. But before I come to that, I must think of God as personal. I have assumed the fact of God so far. For me, God must be at least as much as the farthest reaches of our thought when we speak of personality — a self-conscious Being, a Being of intelligence, of love and of will. I believe man's relation to God is personal, direct, immediate. Is it naïve to record as I did earlier that the Eternal who notes the sparrow's fall knows me, even my name? Some will so regard it. But for me, it is vital.

If I am dealing solely with some vast impersonal force, I might just as well talk about "First Cause," the "Infinite," but I cannot say "Father." All this I learn from Jesus and from experience. I have talked with many men and women of splendid mind, some scientists, some leaders in business and labor, some in government — literary people, thoughtful scholars. These people hold the same faith and would say with me, "God loves" — this I know personally. Do I imagine this? There will be some who will so insist. I do not debate. I have experienced love, the love of father and of mother, of wife and of children. It will be said, "They exist." Yes, they exist. But God exists. This I believe. I said earlier I cannot prove that existence. It posits a problem, I know. But no more difficult for me than many of the problems that are confronted, for instance, in the realm of physics.

The Reverend Ralph W. Sockman in his stimulating volume *How to Believe* quotes the late Professor Eddington of Cambridge, who once said, "I am standing on the threshold about to enter a room. It is a complicated business. In the first place I must shove against an atmosphere pressing with a force of fourteen pounds on every square inch of my body. I must make sure of landing on a plank traveling at twenty miles a second round the sun. I must do this while hanging from a round planet, head outward into space, and with a wind of ether blowing at no one knows how many miles a second through every interstice of my body. The plank has no solidity of substance. To step on it is like stepping on a swarm of flies. Shall I not slip through? Verily it is easier for a camel to pass through the eye of a needle than for a scientific man to pass through a door. And whether this door be a barn door or a church door, it would be wiser that he should consent to be an ordinary man and walk in rather than wait until all the difficulties involved in a scientific ingress are resolved."*

Yes, the Psalmist did consider the heavens and did ask the question, "What is man that Thou are mindful of him?" But it is also true that when I consider the same heavens and the earth, the sunset at evening and the glory of dawn, when I hear the still, small voice, or when I stand alone in the presence of nature — towering mountain and heaving sea — when I look into the eyes of a little child, full of trust, I sense the presence of a greater love, a greater mind, a greater will. When I see that love manifest itself in a breaking through of such a nature that the Eternal takes upon Himself the limitations of humanity that He may be fully understood by the children He has created, for me, at least, I speak of God as

* A. S. Eddington, *Nature of the Physical World* (New York: The Macmillan Company, 1929), p. 342. Ralph W. Sockman, *How to Believe* (New York: Doubleday & Company, Inc., 1953), pp. 39-40.

personal, and believe that my relationship with Him is
personal and direct and immediate.

I am sure that nothing stands between a man and the
Eternal save his own will — neither church, nor clergy,
nor creed. I would be the last to discount church. I believe it to be a divine institution. I would not discount
the profession to which I have given my life. I believe it
to be a sacred calling. I would not discount creed. We
must formulate the faith in as clear a statement as is
possible. But I am sure that God never gave a church,
any church, a monopoly upon the means of grace. Surely
He never gave a humanly limited clerical class authority
to open or close doors to His presence. And no finite
statement can possibly contain all that is to be known
about the infinite. No, nothing can separate a man from
the love of God. There are no toll gates on the King's
highway. That road was opened long since by One who
carried a cross to Calvary. When I know that nothing
can separate me from the love of God, I know that in
all matters affecting my eternal welfare, I am beyond
the reach of any human dictator; I am not dependent
upon any human institution. I can face the future unafraid. I can take anything that may happen to me in the
certainty and the serenity that characterized Jesus.

The remarkable story of Hanns Lilje, Bishop of Han-
nover, former president of the Lutheran World Federation, is told in a little volume entitled *The Valley of the
Shadow*. Bishop Lilje was a prisoner of Hitler. He speaks
of the awful finality of that moment when the steel door
of his cell swung shut — the hardest moment of all,

harder than all the hours and days when death seemed very near. It seems incredible, but they placed fetters upon this man of God at nighttime, chains from his wrists to his ankles. In the daytime they were removed. Once he heard a prisoner whistling far down the cell block, "O for a thousand tongues to sing My great Redeemer's praise." Bishop Lilje writes that he rushed to the bars of his cell and whistled back antiphonally, "O for a thousand tongues to sing."

He tells of Christmas Eve. He thought of his family, of the church, of the sermon he had preached the year before. His text was from the words of the prophet Isaiah, "The people that walked in darkness have seen a great light." The bishop heard his number called. He records that as a rule that meant nothing good. He was taken directly to the commandant, who turned to a guard and said, "Bring number 212 to this cell, too." Number 212 was a great violinist who was under sentence of death. The door was opened and standing before the bishop was a count whom he recognized. He was soon to be executed. Bishop Lilje writes, "At the Commandant's suggestion the violinist played a Christmas chorale, exquisitely: then, in this cell, and before this congregation, I read the Gospel for Christmas Day: 'Now it came to pass in those days there went out a decree . . .' The violinist played another Christmas chorale; in the meantime I had been able to arrange my thoughts a little about the passage in Isaiah which had filled my mind when I was summoned downstairs. I said to my fellow-prisoners: 'This evening we are a congregation, part of the Church of Christ. At this moment in our cells, we have practically nothing that makes the Christmas festival so familiar and so lovely, but there is one thing left to us: God's great promise. Let us cling to this promise, and to Him, in the midst of the darkness. Here and now, in the midst of the uncertainty of our prison life, in the shadow of death, we will praise Him by a firm and unshaken faith in His word, which is addressed to *us*.' Then, in the midst of the cell, the Count knelt down upon the hard stone floor, and while I prayed aloud the beautiful old prayer of confession from Thomas a Kempis (which he himself had chosen) and then pronounced absolution, the tears were running silently down his cheeks. It was a very quiet celebration of the Sacrament full of deep confidence in God; almost palpably the wings of the Divine Mercy hovered over us, as we knelt at the altar in a prison cell on Christmas Eve. We were prisoners, in the power of the Gestapo — in Berlin. But the peace of God enfolded us: it was *real* and present, 'like a Hand laid gently upon us.' "*

Nothing can separate us from the love of God.

In this conception, I find myself a fellow worker with God. "My Father worketh hitherto, and I work." All work becomes sacred. It is God's will I seek to know, God's will I seek to do. There is a moral purpose written into the nature of things.

I may be wrong, but for me, religion really takes off where philosophical speculation ends. Religion is not ar-

* Hanns Lilje, *The Valley of the Shadow* (Philadelphia: The Muhlenberg Press, 1950), pp. 83-84.

gument, it is assurance. William Temple was right when he wrote, "Religion does not consist in supposing that there is a God; it consists in personal trust in God rising to personal fellowship with God." Such an affirmation does not answer the question raised by the Dartmouth senior. Is there reality to correspond with the carefully phrased definitions of the theologian? I believe there is, but can offer no scientific proof. On the other hand, I do not summon you to blind trust, but I stress the fact of trust. We must trust and thrust our lives forward in terms of the faith.

There appears to be a range of power in nature that is guided by perfect intelligence. Temple continued, "We cannot any longer hesitate in supposing that behind the world of nature there is at work a power, guided by principles such as those which also appear in our own minds. The two correspond." * I have already said that the intelligence at work in the universe is, for the man of religion, righteous. Browning put it, "The All Great is the All Loving too."

There is a consciousness of obligation present in all of us, and that obligation is binding, too, upon the Eternal, the Being who is truly morally obligated. Now this is hypothesis, I know. It is the hypothesis upon which the man of religion proceeds, namely, that the power upon which the universe depends, a power guided by perfect intelligence, is the real source of moral aspiration and has a sense of duty. I do not debate this

* William Temple, *Basic Convictions* (New York: Harper & Brothers, 1936), pp. 4, 7.

proposition. This power is finally subordinate to love.
God is love.

Niebuhr suggests that "religion is the self's commitment to some system of meaning, or its loyalty to some
scheme of values." Yes, but to me it is more. I speak as
a Christian. Dr. Niebuhr was thinking of religion —
all religion. For me, religion is commitment to the God
revealed by Jesus. It is commitment to Christ Himself,
since the Christian faith has always held that God was in
Christ reconciling the world unto Himself, that, as Jesus
said, "I and my Father are one." It is really becoming a
new man in Christ Jesus.

It is recorded that Augustine when leaving Africa for
Italy was accosted by his friend Marcianus. Augustine
was still the profligate. Satiated with the sensual, he was
seeking the spiritual. Marcianus said to him as he
walked up the gangplank, "This day that brings another
life to thee demands that thou another man must be."
Augustine never forgot it. Later, after hearing Ambrose
preach in Milan, and after, when pacing up and down
in a garden, he heard someone say, "Take up and read,"
he, having read the words of the Apostle Paul, "Put ye
on the Lord Jesus Christ," did indeed become a new
man in Christ Jesus.

That the power exists, whether personal or impersonal, most intelligent men believe. Einstein, who possessed one of the great minds of history, and to whom
the world owes so much, turns from his contemplation of
the universe to speak of "the grandeur of reason incarnate." He held that this grandeur "in its profoundest

depths is inaccessible to man." The humility that is developed in the presence of this grandeur is for him "religion in the highest sense of the word." He said, "Whoever has undergone the intense experience of successful advances in the domain of scientific thought is moved by profound reverence for the rationality made manifest in existence." He seemed to think that if the relationship were personal, it involved the interference by God in the regularity of events at the request of some person who implored God to postpone the sunrise to an hour that was more suitable. He called upon religious leaders to give up the doctrine of a personal God. It was this doctrine, he thought, that placed power in the hands of the priest, since it was assumed the priest used his office to effect the change.

Einstein did not understand the doctrine of a personal God. He saw in the doctrine a crude anthropomorphism. The argument he sought to destroy would be rejected by thoughtful theologians. He saw solace in the conception of an omnipotent, just, and omni-beneficent personal God, but he felt that such a concept made God responsible for every act of every person, and in a sense God could not hold men responsible for their acts, because this was to sit really in judgment upon Himself, who was really responsible. That there are problems here, no one will deny. The genius of Einstein that could see "the grandeur of reason incarnate" is matched in religion by the genius of prophet and priest who, contemplating the same universe, have experienced "the glory of love infinite." The Christian sings, "Love so amazing, so divine, demands my soul, my life, my all."

Is it naïve to hold that a mind like Einstein's that could think God's thoughts — no matter how restricted the area — is to be met by a mind that can be described both as "reason incarnate" and as "love infinite"?

I believe in God. I can do no other. It is impossible for me to consider the heavens, to study nature, to contemplate the order and the law everywhere present without reaching the conclusion that there is intelligence back of it all. The chances are so overwhelming against chance that I cannot believe that the law that operates in the universe and in the atom is but a fortuitous concourse of circumstances. Nor do I find answer in materialism. To me, right or wrong, I must start with mind. From all I see, this mind appears to operate upon principles that can be understood by intelligence. It is intelligible. There seems to be a law of reason valid for all human minds which I believe operates in the case of God Himself. I would bow in reverent respect before such a mind if it were but intelligence. But for me, it must be more than that. It must be love, perfect love, righteous love. God must be at least as much as what we mean when we use the term personality. He may be much, much more; but He must be that. Unless there can be a relationship that is personal, then there is no relationship at all. He must know that He is being worshiped, and the worshiper must know that God knows. When I bow in prayer and say, "Our Father," it must be more than a kind of self-hypnotism through which I convince myself that I am important in the sight of the Eternal. Jesus believed the relationship was so personal that in an exclamation of poetic splendor He thought of the hairs of the head as being numbered. The God who clothes the lily in raiment unsurpassed by Solomon in all his glory knows our needs. He knows each one of us. This is not the relationship of a cringing being, groveling in the presence of omnipotence. On the contrary, it is a being of infinite worth and of great dignity, standing in the presence of his Creator, certain of the Creator's love, a son before a Father. This I believe. Prove it? I cannot. Act upon it, I can.

It is precisely at the point of action that I am most deeply concerned. As a minister, I have noted the awful abyss that at times separates the conduct of the person who affirms the Creed on Sunday and bows God out of his activities on Monday. I do not mean the person who indulges in gross immorality, the man who steals, profanes, degrades. I refer to the man who stands well in the community, who is regarded as a good citizen, dresses well, speaks well, lives well. He is a man who is fearful of communism, and understandably so. He talks about Marxian atheism and its threat to the free society, and rightly so.

Atheistic communism is seen as striking at all he holds dear, and it does. But he appears to be unaware of a practical atheism no less dangerous. It is the atheism that bows God out of normal practice; the atheism that never asks, "Is this course of action in accord with God's will?" It is an atheism that yesterday could corner the wheat market. What did God have to do with the market place! God is worshiped in church, not on the floor of the wheat exchange! That practice has given way before the theism that demands morality, and a man who would corner the wheat market today would not be called a genius, he would be called a gangster. But what about profiteering, condemned in war, now boasted about as evidence of the success of businessmen in government? This is not to condemn the profit system. It is to ask what God's will is in the matter of fortunes built up almost overnight through the exploitation of natural resources. I do not condemn. I speak as one who has sinned. It may prove to be wiser to keep alive the drive that emerges from the pursuit of self-interest. There is a dead hand placed upon the society in which regulation and control have gone to the place where creativity is stifled. But what is God's will in a situation where an uneducated man who farms a poor piece of land and barely ekes out a living suddenly hears there is oil beneath the surface or radioactive ore upon his property? He leases the property and a vast fortune pours into his bank account. It is his, we say. And it is. Is stewardship or its denial the answer? A teacher instructs succeeding generations of students. He earns a few thousand dollars a year, and having produced the truest of wealth, enlightened character, he dies with a small pension fund for his wife, a bit of property. Is that the way it should be? Artists often starve, until some promoter dealer creates a demand for a particular school, buys up the canvases, sells them for fabulous prices. What about the millions of Asia, a large percentage of whom go to bed hungry, or throw themselves down upon some dirty mat in a hovel at night? Do we wait until the Communist comes with his declaration, "We have the way to abolish the exploitation of man by man. We can establish the classless society. We speak as scientists, not as purveyors of opium who in the name of religion fasten the chains upon your ankles. United, you have nothing to lose but your chains?" Personally, I believe he will lead the people to the desert rather than to the promised land. But what has all this to do with God? Are we really our brother's keeper? Was Jesus right when He told us to leave our gifts at the altar and go out and be right with our brother, if that brother had aught against us? When we say, "Thy will be done," what do we mean? Do we really take God into consideration? Is it not almost blasphemy when we preen ourselves in God's sun, and announce that we have prayer services in the nation's Capitol, and then vote measures that sell the people's birthright to those who come bringing the steaming mess of pottage?

It is a practical atheism that constitutes a real threat. We break God's laws at our peril. Why doesn't He step in and take over? Why not another flood, a few selected for another ark, and a new start? There is no answer there. God must give man freedom of choice or man ceases to be responsible. Man is free. Free to destroy his life; free to commit sin; and out of his freedom come war, and vice, and exploitation. Could God do other? I think not. Automatons or moral robots are no more than machines. But man created in the image of God, God's son, that is something different. God's will must be made known, His love fully shown, His forgiveness offered. The great event of creation must be matched by an equally great event, the act of redemption. Is it possible for man to receive the power to walk in the Way, the Truth, and the Life? The Christian religion so believes. It has thus centered upon regeneration, a new spirit, rather than upon revolution or reform, a new society; not because it rejects the new society — on the contrary, it demands it — but because it sees the new man in Christ Jesus as antecedent to the new society, which is the Kingdom of God.

Years ago I sat in a class in Systematic Theology and studied under a great teacher. We considered the attributes of God. It was clear enough that He must have all power, omnipotence; that He must be everywhere present, omnipresence; that He must have all knowledge, omniscience. It seemed evident that He must be personal, and if to be worshiped, must be moral. But for me, these attributes, which I admitted — I had to — did not add up to the Being I needed and who I believed must exist. I knew there was more than my eye could see. I never heard a song without knowing someone had written the lyrics and someone had composed the music, or at least that many had sung and out of the folk repetition of melody and the growth of harmony, the song of the people had come. When Mother read stories, I knew someone had written them. I saw paintings. Some of the earliest prints I saw at school were from Millet, *The*

Sower and *The Angelus*. I knew there was a peasant painter in France. And even as a boy, I knew there was someone who cared for sun, moon, and stars, the seas, the cattle upon a thousand hills. Yes, my father prayed:

> O God, our help in ages past,
> Our hope for years to come . . .

I knew there was a God. I know it now. I cannot prove it. But I try to live in terms of the faith. I find the faith presents fewer problems than the lack of it. The answer of the materialist does not satisfy. It does not meet the needs of the intellect. It does not satisfy, because it does not meet the facts. There is more truth, at least it seems so to me, in the answer that involves a Supreme Being, intelligent, at once all-powerful and all-loving, a Father who seeks His children, and, as I believe, One who took the great step necessary to make Himself known, His will understood — in a word, One who revealed Himself in a person. At least, this is my faith. I am less concerned about arguing; I prefer affirmation. Test out the affirmation and see whether it works. This is the principle upon which I prefer to proceed. "I believe in God, the Father Almighty." This belief satisfies my mind and when tested out in conduct, meets the needs of my heart. I believe such procedure is in keeping with that of the great men of science who seek the explanation most rational for the facts that are before them. This is the best explanation for me, and projecting my life forward upon such a faith, I find intellectual peace, moral satisfaction, and, what is equally important, power — flowing from the faith that enables one to face the morrow, eyes front, and in the certainty that all is well.

CHAPTER II

I Believe in Jesus Christ

IN RELIGION, experience is more important than explanation. A man stands enthralled as the rising sun transforms the desert. Black night gives way to morning ablaze in color, and the silences become song. He talks of the sunrise. Quite properly he may seek explanation of the glory of the dawn. He turns to physicist, botanist, biologist, and geologist and learns of light and life and the earth's story. That is all right. But if his interest in explanation becomes so acute that he no longer rises before the sun to stand in the darkness and await the first carmine line that delineates the mountain ridge — in a word, if he no longer experiences the sunrise — explanation becomes substitute for experience, and the search for explanation has taken from him the experience for which he sought explanation.

So, too, in the case of Jesus. I have studied and have

listened to the explanations. The Nicene Creed gives with one hand and takes away with the other, striving for a balanced explanation — Very God and Very Man, made, but not made! From some points of view, Christology is the most important theme to which the mind of man can direct itself. But christological theory is like the explanation of the sunrise. Experience is often lost in explanation.

"I believe . . . in Jesus Christ, His only Son our Lord." I repeat that honestly, reverently, without mental reservation of any kind; and there is an inner glow when I utter the words. I do so believe.

"But do you believe in the Virgin Birth?" someone asks. Historically speaking, the inclusion of this affirmation in the Creed was more a matter of proving the humanity of Jesus than of affirming His divinity. Unless one is familiar with the theological debate of the first and second centuries, it may come as a surprise to learn that there were many who doubted the reality of Christ's earthly life. Marcion, for instance, denied absolutely that Jesus had been born of a woman. There were denials of the material reality of Christ's body. There were those who insisted that Christ was a spiritual being, absolutely distinct from the man Jesus. I am not interested in the historical debate of centuries gone by in the present discussion, but must point out that the inclusion of the phrase "born of the Virgin Mary" had more to do with the reality than with the uniqueness of our Lord's birth.

In those days, it is true that when men sought to account for genius, they thought it necessary to attribute to genius some miraculous occurrence in order to explain it. Jesus was not the only one alleged to have been virgin born. Many volumes have been written upon the question of the Virgin Birth. The purpose of the doctrine has been to stress the sinlessness of Jesus, to affirm His spiritual purity and moral perfection. It is offensive to me to assume that there is something sinful in the love and the act that result in procreation. The doctrine assumes that Jesus was conceived without sin, and this means without a human father. I refuse to believe that there is sin in the form of conception that God Himself has ordained for humanity.

The deityship of Jesus rests on firmer ground, in my thinking, than upon the idea of virgin birth so prevalent in centuries gone by. The author of the article on "The Virgin Birth" in the *Encyclopedia of Religion and Ethics* begins by saying, "A wonder birth or a supernatural birth is one of the commonest ideas in folk-tale and myth." It is true that these accounts differ from that of the Virgin Birth because they allege that a god was the father of the person alleged to be divine. Plato and Augustus were said to be sons of Apollo; and it was argued that the kings of Egypt were sons of a god and a human mother. There is, of course, difference of opinion as to the legends that Zoroaster was virgin born, and in all probability the stories associated with Buddha are mythical. Nonetheless, attempts to account for genius were often buttressed by affirmations of miraculous birth.

I do not mean to debate this question, but I find it

difficult to confront the fact that Jesus Himself never mentioned it. When He called His disciples, He did not inquire, "Do you believe I was virgin born?" No, He said, "Follow me." His brother James is silent upon the question. Surely James would have said something about it, had it been a vital matter at the time. Peter, first among the apostles crucified in the name of his Lord, does not ask the early Christian, "Is your faith grounded in the doctrine of the Virgin Birth?" And John, the disciple closest to our Lord, John the spiritual, John who taught Christ's deity more convincingly than any other, what does he say? Nothing! But more important than all of this is the silence of Paul, the theologian; Paul, the founder of the Church.

Now, I do not say these men rejected the doctrine. I do say that this part of the explanation of Jesus appears to have been of such minor significance that they neither stressed the doctrine nor required its acceptance to become Christians. I do not here refer to the meaning of the word "virgin" as used in other parts of the Bible, or to the problem of tracing the lineage of Jesus through Joseph. I am trying to say that the never-ending attempted explanations that never really explain sometimes miss the experience.

I am not lightly tossing aside the word of scholars. I am talking about my own personal faith in Christ. The lesser miracles do not impress me as does the great miracle, the miracle expressive of the overwhelming love of God, the breaking through of the Eternal in a Person so that we may truly apprehend God and know Him.

Ideas are meaningful for most men when beheld incarnate in other men. If we would know the meaning of an idea, we must see it alive in a person.

At the heart of the Christian faith is the doctrine of the Incarnation. It is held that God took upon Himself the limitations of humanity so that He might be known in a Person. We hold that the ultimate became intimate, that perfection came alive in personality, that the Word became flesh and dwelt among us. This, of course, is a great leap of faith, but it is one that for me is not difficult. "God so loved the world that He gave His only begotten Son." It was out of love that Jesus came. The God Jesus revealed was a God of love. I can understand so much better when I turn to Jesus. I can live by the experience of God as found in Jesus.

This question came up some time ago during a conference with a group of men in a great city of the South. Some of these men were certain that Methodism was being subverted by bishops who they were convinced were Communists. I thought of a card a friend had given me. It read, "My mind is made up already. Don't confuse me with facts." Some of these men were convinced the World Council of Churches and the National Council of Churches were almost Communist fronts. The fact that the presidents of the World Council at that time were the Archbishop of Canterbury, who crowned Elizabeth Queen of England; Bishop Berggrav, former Primate of the Norwegian Church, who had fearlessly faced the Nazis and had suffered imprisonment; Pastor Marc Boegner of France, president of the Protestant French Federation, whose life has been a spiritual blessing and whose courage an inspiration; Sarah Chakko, the outstanding Christian woman and educator of Asia; and Archbishop Athenagoras of the Greek Orthodox Church; the fact that Moscow papers at the very moment were insisting that the World Council was a tool of Wall Street because of the prominence of Mr. John Foster Dulles at Amsterdam; the fact that some of the outstanding Christian laymen of the nation, leaders of American enterprise, were members of the General Board of the National Council of Churches meant nothing. These little men knew. The source of their knowledge was of course confidential; it was classified secret — top secret — but there was no question as to its authenticity.

After I had presented the facts concerning the World Council of Churches and the National Council of Churches of Christ, the very first question was phrased in accusation form: "You do not believe in the Immaculate Conception, do you?" I replied, "Of course not." I then went on, "The very fact you have asked this question shows that you are not qualified to ask questions in the field of theology. No Methodist believes in the Immaculate Conception. No Protestant does. Actually the doctrine of the Immaculate Conception is a Roman Catholic doctrine, not proclaimed until 1854, and must not be confused, as you have done, with the doctrine of the Virgin Birth. It has to do with Mary and not with Jesus." It was a doctrine that was affirmed at last after centuries of discussion, a doctrine opposed by Thomas Aquinas himself. There were theological reasons that caused ecclesiastics to insist upon its declaration. Actually, it meant simply that the Virgin Mary from the first instant of her conception was preserved "from all stain of original sin." When I pointed this out, the questioner was irritated. Ignorance when exposed soon moves to anger. It is seldom happy in receiving truth.

The point I am trying to stress is that when we wander off into the deserts of dry explanation we separate ourselves from the life-giving waters of experience.

There are those who also raise a query the moment one affirms, "I believe . . . in Jesus Christ, His only Son our Lord." They ask, "And was He not a sacrifice for the sins of the whole world, satisfying a deity who demanded payment for sin if man were to be saved from eternal damnation?"

I have never been able to carry the idea of justice to the place where someone else can vicariously pay for what I have done in order to clean the slate. There is always, too, the further question, "Was His payment one that satisfies the demands of a bookkeeping deity for all time? Past sins and all future sins, too? Is it thus that God is reconciled?" God is just. I believe that. But God is love. I know that. When the Prodigal Son came home, it was love that compelled the father to rush down the road to receive that wayward boy to his heart. There is nothing there of payment for the substance spent in riotous living. Of course, the boy lost those years in his father's house. He did eat the husks fed to swine, and he did expect to become as one of his father's hired servants. But as Jesus Himself tells the story, this is not the course it takes. A purple robe is put upon him, a ring upon his finger; the family makes merry, the son is home again. It has always seemed to me that love is a sufficient explanation of the father's conduct. That is the way a being of love acts. When a man comes to himself, when he repents and seeks forgiveness, love stands with open arms and joyful heart. At least that is the way it has seemed to me.

Now I know that, reading the same Scriptures, Roman Catholic and Protestant scholars and the great minds of Orthodoxy have come to different conclusions relative to the plan of salvation. I know there are contradictory theories of the atonement. Doctrines must be understood in terms of the thought forms of the day they emerged. We speak of Jesus as King of kings and Lord of lords. Obviously, we are thinking out of the day when there were kings and lords. When I repeat, "Jesus Christ is to become Ruler of the kings of the earth," a statement that I do repeat with assurance, I am adopting, of course, phraseology that would not have emerged in a democracy. It comes from monarchy, from feudalism. So, too, in the case of the atonement. There was a time when men sought to propitiate the gods with sacrifices. These sacrifices ran the gamut from sheep and goats to human beings.

I shall never forget the sense of shame that stole over me at Khali-ghat Temple in Calcutta. I saw the goats and sheep being led to slaughter. The poor animals seemed to know they were to die, and in pitiful bleating struggled against the ropes that dragged them to their death. What kind of god is it that demands such sacrifices? I thought of the Abraham story and the moment when Abraham was about to slay his own son as a sacrifice. He thought God had so commanded him. No wonder the prophets of Israel cried out:

I hate, I despise your feasts,
And I will not smell the savor of your festivals,
And with your cereal offerings I will not be pleased,
And the peace offerings of your fatlings I will not
    regard with favor.
Banish from me the noise of your songs,
For to the melody of your lyres I will not listen.
But let justice roll on as a flood of waters,
And righteousness like an unfailing stream.

In English history, there was a time when everything had a money tag upon it. A cow, a sheep, a horse, but also a man, a servant, a free man! If one were killed, the killer had to pay the price. That was it. It, in a sense, was the old eye for an eye and a tooth for a tooth.

That man sins no one will deny. We have all come short of the glory of God. But that a curse is upon man because of the sin of the first man is to me an immoral absurdity. I am not responsible personally for Adam's sin or for Cain's murder. Doctrines of original sin, when properly developed, hedged here and there, strung out endlessly, may make sense; and I would be the very last to discount the terrible fact of sin. But to me, it is easier to say that man given freedom of choice does choose wrong; and since I find the essence of sin in selfishness and rebellion against the will of God, I know that man stands in the need not only of prayer but of salvation. When I read history and behold man's inhumanity to man, witness torture in the name of religion and of law, and torture for no other purpose than to maim or to slay — yes, we have sinned. All are sinners, and redemption is a fundamental necessity. This is not the issue. I deal with something else. Theologians have spun out answers in the thought molds of certain days, and many insist upon holding to ancient phrasing that becomes less and less meaningful in our day.

For instance, I must read in the beautiful service of Holy Communion about the sacrifice of my Blessed Lord — "who made there, by the one offering of Himself, a full, perfect, and sufficient sacrifice for the sins of the whole world." I believe He did, but not as some hold. They think of a tight little legal setup, so much sin, so much payment. It is too much like the money price that was upon a slave or a beast, the price that had to be paid were either killed. Such people, seeking to find an exact price, soon realize that the sin is so great that no one can satisfy a judge who demands payment to the last farthing. But they insist there must be payment, and argue that God sent His own Son, who died upon the Cross and in so doing satisfied God's sense of legalistic justice. They hold that this sacrifice was sufficient to get the accounts straight, to rule off debits against this great credit, a sufficient payment for all of the past and for all of the days to come. It simply does not make sense to me. It is rather an offense. It offends my moral sense.

Of course, God cannot condone sin. Sin does make a difference. God cannot forgive men who have committed crime unless they have repented of the crime. To forgive sinful men while they remain sinful would in itself be immoral. Some way must be found whereby unrighteous and immoral men may become righteous and moral. It is therefore primarily a question of the relation of the individual to God, not a legal transaction, at least so it seems to me. I can never forget the affirmation, "By grace are ye saved." I have to deal not with sin in the abstract but with sinners who are human beings. I simply cannot think of the divine family and the divine Father and then set the family up upon the basis of a terrible judge who could not so much as forgive his children without some payment for sin which they themselves were unable to meet. As I say, God cannot condone sin. A man is responsible for his acts; otherwise, he is not free. This is the basis of law in a free society. If I steal, I break the law and there is penalty. I am sentenced. If I murder, it may mean I must pay with my life. But must God have a sacrifice, the Lamb slain from the beginning of the foundation of the world, as the Book says?

No, no, I cannot think of it this way. I see Jesus as God's Son; I have no trouble with the concept of deity. The essential truth of the incarnation is what the word itself means, God incarnate, incarnate in a Person. That Person had limitations. I believe Christ really suffered. I do not think that this was part of a predetermined drama wherein the great Playwright set down the lines to be repeated, with the player, in this case Christ, moving here

and there as the Director ordered, the end known from
the beginning. It is almost blasphemous for someone to
say that this is so and that the Cross was simply a part of
the act. No, for me it was a real cross, it was Roman
torture without refinement. When Jesus prayed in
Gethsemane, "May this cup pass from me," He meant it.
But God's will, whatever that will demanded, was to be
done. That was Christ's determination. When He hung
from that cross and cried, "My God, why hast Thou for-
saken me?" surely this was not a bit of a drama, fore-
seen; it was the cry of a man well-nigh brokenhearted.
Yes, God was in Christ, reconciling the world unto Himself. This I believe. That reconciliation lay in the revelation of a Being of ineffable love. Jesus endured the Cross
to reveal that love, and by His example so moved in
upon the heart of humanity and in upon my heart that
I realize it was for me He died, for me, so that I may
know God and His love, a love that sent the Son, a love
that was incarnate in the Son, a love that overrules my
own selfishness, a love that evokes a repentance that in
itself is sufficient for the Being I worship and adore. His
righteousness does not demand dollars, or goats, or even
the death of His dear Son, except as that death is the occasion of my changed heart. Yes, as it is in the hymn, this
love demands my all.

I know some will say this is to abandon a cardinal
doctrine of faith. I think not. I have just looked through
a great tome entitled *System of Christian Doctrine.* I
can see the scholarly old teacher as he expounded the
various conceptions of the atonement. I rejoice that

while he did not put the case as I have, he did make
clear the weakness, not to say the immorality, of a legalistic doctrine that calls for someone to atone for my sins
and all sins, in order to satisfy a Being who demands
legalistic justice. Personally, I believe the love of God
responds to the repentant sinner, and forgiveness does
follow. I do not think telling beads or going on pilgrim-
ages or relying upon someone else to pay for me does it.
No, it was "amazing grace, how sweet the sound!" Yes,
He died for me, and for every man, not to pay an angry
God but to overwhelm me with irresistible love, showing
me the Father's heart and summoning me to the Father's
house. He is my Saviour.

I must accept the God of love by faith. I am utterly
unworthy. The love Jesus revealed compels me. I cannot
resist it — although many do. I think this love fails to
reach many because we present it so poorly.

I behold that love when I see Jesus. Picture Jesus
teaching. See Him sitting upon a great stone beneath a
tree, about Him an eager crowd listening intently. He
taught as one having authority. A little child stands on
the outer edge of the crowd. She is caught by His voice;
perhaps she has been able to see His eyes. She breaks the
stem of a Palestinian lily, makes her way in and out
among the older people, and is about to present the
flower to Him. Was it then that someone sought to re-
strain her? I do not know. Perhaps Jesus said, "Suffer the
little children to come unto Me, and forbid them not:
for of such is the kingdom of heaven." In any case, I
am sure if such a child had come to Jesus, He would

have reached out His arms to her, and she would have rushed to Him. I think He would have said, "What is your name?" If she had answered, "My name is Mary," I am sure He would have said, "That is a beautiful name. That is my mother's name." She might have given Him the flower, and had she done so, I think Jesus would have asked, "Mary, do you know who takes care of the flowers?" If she had said no, I think He would have told her of the One who cares for the flowers but who cares infinitely more for every child upon the face of the earth — black, white, red, yellow, brown. God is like that. I can understand that.

Or again, I see Him in the city streets. A woman is kneeling in the center of a crowd of men. She has made a mistake, they say, and in accordance with the law, they are going to stone her. I cannot think of a meek and lowly Jesus at such a moment, but I see God's Son, with eyes flashing, stepping into that crowd of cowards — mobs are always made up of cowards — and saying to the hypocrites, "If any one of you has not sinned, you cast a stone at her, will you?" Before long, they have gone, hiding the stones in their robes. At last, Jesus, looking down, says, "Woman, where art thine accusers?" She looks up. "Lord, they have all gone." I hear His never-to-be-forgotten words: "Neither do I condemn you. Go your way and sin no more." God is like that. I can understand that.

And again, in the Garden when facing the Cross, Jesus, with disciples too weary to keep awake, prays alone that the cup might pass from Him. Loving life even as we love it, He finally declares, "Not my will but Thine be done." One realizes that God Himself suffers. He has to deal with us, and finding us as we are, He suffers.

There comes the closing moment upon the Cross, the crowd jeering, and some rough person shouting to the dying Saviour, "Well, if you are a god, why don't you come down?" We hear a prayer that has echoed through the centuries and will be repeated through all the centuries to come: "Father, forgive them, for they know not what they do." God is like that.

Is the universe like that? Does God's love cease to operate after a few short years? A man is reared in bad environment, inherits a poor body, becomes a criminal, hates, kills, dies. Perhaps all this before he is twenty! Is the God of Jesus One who condemns for all eternity a man who has lived but two decades? Another child is reared in a Christian home, experiences love, is well educated. Doors open for him and he serves splendidly, dies at eighty, respected and loved. He moves into eternity, according to some, to experience bliss forever and forever. Is it the same God of love who is related to each one of these? Is God an Accountant who demands reparation, crediting good deeds — no, no. It is by faith we are saved, we say. Is God a Being who must have the accounts squared by some death, the sacrifice of a Son even, that the individual's account may be ruled off in two red lines, the balance in sin paid by a being who died long since and left a great control account from which the Deity may draw forever? Frankly, such doctrines do not help me.

I am helped when I turn to Jesus repentant, conscious of sin, seeking forgiveness. I find in Him God manifest in a Person. He is for me the Way, the Truth, the Life. When He says, "Follow me," He makes it abundantly clear that if I am to follow Him, I must love Him, and if I love Him, I must keep His commandments. He tells me that he who would be greatest among us must become servant of all and insists that inasmuch as we do it unto the least of these, we do it unto Him. "This is my Father's house," He says. He searches for the lost sheep, the lost coin, the lost son, and all of this out of love. Yes, there is a pearl of great price. The wise man will sell all to possess it.

No, I do not think of Him as a moralist. I do not think He could have separated Himself from the world and been content to write a book on conduct or the rules of spiritual living for the guidance of humanity. He was what He taught. For me, He is God with us. I believe that He and the Father were one. I believe He is God's Son. "I believe . . . in Jesus Christ, His only Son our Lord." I know this may be as difficult for some as Virgin Birth, Atonement, Descent into Hell, and all the rest of the explanations, but it is not for me.

I am sure a God of love would seek, constantly seek, to make Himself known to His children. The relation of father and child is personal. The love must be experienced. Is God a Christlike God? This I believe. Some of the explainers force me to cry out, as did Mary, "They have taken away my Lord, and I do not know where they have laid Him."

In Jesus, I see God as One who sees in every man a

son, a being of infinite worth. Jesus addressed God as "Father." He did not begin the Lord's Prayer with "Your August Majesty" or "Your Holiness" or "Your Beatitude." The salutation was very simple, "Our Father." Our, all of us. Father, Creator, One who loves His children — each one of us, black, red, brown, yellow, white — created by the same Being, each a child of God and each a member of God's family and therefore brothers. Our forefathers held to this, too. "Endowed by the Creator with certain unalienable rights." Endowed with them. They cannot be alienated. The state does not confer our liberties; it merely confirms them. They belong to us because we are sons of God. I stand straighter and walk with surer stride. I know I am a son of God, a being of awful dignity, for whom God went so far as to send His Son that I might experience God's love.

In Jesus, I see a God whose love is unfailing, who causes the sun to shine upon the just and the unjust alike. Bishop Francis John McConnell once said, "I would hate to trust some men I know with the sunshine." But God's love is infinite; it reaches sinner and saint, Jew and Gentile, black and white, all of His children. When Hosea's wife proved unfaithful and the home was broken, Hosea, who loved Gomer, finally could stand the separation no longer. He loved her. She was returned to his home, and he, pondering the experience, realizing his own shortcomings, suddenly grasped a sublime truth: "If I, Hosea, can forgive an unfaithful wife, I, with my sins and limitations, what about God Himself? Does He love to the uttermost? Is He not willing to forgive? His is a love that never fails." No wonder Paul could say, "Nothing can separate us from the love of God which is in Christ Jesus."

In Jesus I see God as the sustainer of the universe, of the lilies of the field, the stars and the skies, of blades of grass, trees, and as One who counts the hairs of a child's head. God is back of the regularities of the universe. The sun will rise tomorrow morning, the earth will rotate, the laws are maintained. I can count on God. My problem is, can He count on me?

In Jesus I see a God brokenhearted by the son who is alienated, and ever waiting for his return, unwilling to coerce but always ready to forgive. How many fathers have seen their sons do wrong and, headstrong, leave home and start for the far country. Some of them do feed eventually upon the husks that swine eat. But there comes a day. Yes, God suffers. The shepherd searches for the lost sheep, even though ninety-nine are in the fold. He searches and finds the sheep, and by that time it is willing to be carried back to the sheepfold. The love of God reaches down and the lost son refuses to respond. God is limited by His very nature, by His own laws. He will not force repentance. Just as He cannot by His nature do an immoral thing, neither can He break His own laws and take from the boy the power to say no to God. But God seeks, never ceasing.

In Jesus I see a God who understands the heart of a penitent prostitute and the hypocrisy of the religious men of His day. "If any of you has not sinned," said Jesus. The God Jesus revealed is done once and for all with sham and hypocrisy. We study the history of England or of Italy or, for that matter, any land. How often we behold prelates becoming political officials, power-mad men who justify conduct at once illegal and immoral on the specious plea that it furthers the interests of the Church. The Christ I know cries out, "Woe unto you, scribes and Pharisees, hypocrites!" Speak softly, we are told! Is that soft speech? But even this God, offended in such fashion, would nonetheless gather the people of Jerusalem to Him as a hen gathers her chickens, but, as Jesus put it, "Ye would not."

In Jesus I see a God who is just, who properly estimates the worth of a widow's mite, whose eyes see platters that are unclean and tombs that are full of dead men's bones. Yes, a God of justice. He judged. We are warned, "Judge not," but the Judge of all judges aright. A widow's mite — He knew how much it was worth. He also understood prayers that were but pretense.

In Jesus I see a God who pities, whose Son in the agony of the crucifixion reveals the essential character of God in a prayer that is love incarnate.

"I believe . . . in Jesus Christ, His only Son our Lord." As I said, I have no trouble with the doctrine of the deityship of Jesus. I really believe that God Himself uniquely revealed Himself in Jesus. The Christian faith has always conceived of Jesus as both God and man. He was tempted even as we are tempted. He suffered. He hungered and was athirst. It is just this that makes Christianity the one religion for me. I respect all other religions. I believe in religious liberty. But I do not equate all religions. I do not believe one religion is as good as another. I believe that God once acted to make Himself fully known. He could have done it in other ways, no doubt, but He chose this way. At least that is my belief. Obviously God did not grow in wisdom and in stature and in favor with God and man. The All Knowing could not have been the partially knowing at one time. Mystery, yes! Difficult to explain, yes! But not too difficult. I believe God could have chosen to make himself known. I believe He did. If He so exalted man as to choose a human being for such revelation, that adds to the glorious dignity of man. But that He could, I do not doubt. That He did, I believe. I think of Jesus as the God-man. The limitations of humanity, yes! The glory of God, yes! God can manifest Himself in many ways. We believe He manifested Himself in Jesus and continues to manifest Himself in a Spirit, ever present. We speak of God the Father, God the Son, God the Holy Spirit. And now I have raised the question of the Trinity. I have read and read, but never a completely satisfying explanation. That I experience God as Father, Son, and Holy Spirit I know. But explain? I cannot.

All of this is to suggest my own inability to go with the explainers and to understand as I go. It is not to suggest lack of faith, sincere faith in Jesus Christ, God's Son, God incarnate, the Saviour of the World. Not a Saviour thought of as offering a Shylockian pound of flesh to a Shylockian God; but a Saviour, God with us, so revealing God that we turn in repentance, crying for forgiveness, receiving it in love abounding, moving out to live in that love and to do the will of the Father. "I believe . . . in Jesus Christ, His only Son our Lord." I see Jesus as an act of God, God Himself entering history in the only way that I can conceive the Eternal could truly make Himself fully known, namely, in a Person. Thus I join the Church Universal in a glorious *Adoramus Te:* "I do adore Thee, O Christ, and magnify Thy holy name."

"I believe . . . in Jesus Christ, His only Son our Lord."

CHAPTER III

I Believe in Life Everlasting

IF A MAN die, shall he live again? The question was asked centuries ago by the author of Job; it was asked thousands of years before that; it is asked today; and it will be asked tomorrow.

Omar Khayyám ridiculed the notion. He wrote:

> Ah, my Belovèd, fill the Cup that clears
> Today of past Regrets and future Fears:
> *Tomorrow!* — Why, Tomorrow I may be
> Myself with Yesterday's Sev'n thousand Years.

Omar saw the future as "dust unto dust and under dust to lie," and spoke of those "we loved, the loveliest and the best," who "have drunk their Cup a round or two — and one by one crept silently to rest." He saw saint and savior alike: "Their words to scorn are scattered, and their mouths are stopped with dust." Perhaps

Omar knows better now, but when he was here, he could but cry, "Fools! Your reward is neither here nor there."

Are the words spoken as we lay our dead away but sorry delusion? At the beginning of my ministry, there were times when I wondered, perhaps doubted. When I thought of the relative size of the earth in the universe and tried to comprehend the statements of the astronomers who talked in terms of light years and of incredible distances, who pushed out beyond our own sun and the solar system to blazing stars, to systems beyond systems, to suns we have never seen whose light is still coming toward us but is as yet not discerned, I asked myself, can it be true that the Eternal is really concerned about each tiny being called man? Is it not closer to the fact, I reasoned, to speak of the grass that flourisheth and is cut down? Is it really true that the Lord is my shepherd, that I shall dwell in the house of the Lord forever? What did Jesus mean when He spoke of His Father's house with its many mansions and places He has prepared for us?

I little realized then that I was trying to compare what cannot be compared. I know little about heat and light and the constitution of matter. I use such terms as "electrons" and speak of "atomic energy." These are commonplaces of current conversation, easily repeated, but understood by few. For me, there is a fundamental difference between matter and mind. There is little point in discussing the weight of the earth or attempts to measure the speed with which this planet rotates upon its axis or whirls through space when we are talking about personality. We cannot add pounds and yards; this we know. Nor can we equate stars and souls. Stars there are, and infinite distances, but what have these to do with the human soul, with personality?

There is no affirmation in the Creed that I repeat with greater assurance today than that of the climaxing declaration: "I believe in . . . the life everlasting." The Christian believes we are living forever now. Man is immortal.

During World War II, I flew over the Anzio beachhead. I looked down upon that costly bit of sand. It made me think of a face that had suffered from smallpox. The German fire was so intense that every square yard had been churned up and the beach was pockmarked. Later, when the forces moved to the north, I walked over these sands with my younger son. He said, "Dad, I will take you to my foxhole." I replied, "Nonsense, you cannot find a foxhole upon a beachhead like this." He said quietly, "If you had been here for three and a half months, you could find it." We did. Then after we had taken a few pictures, he said, "Dad, I want you to come with me to the cemetery." It is nearby at a place called Nettuno. Nine thousand five hundred crosses are there.

He took me to one cross and said, "Dad, would you read a prayer here?" I said, "Why here?" Pointing to the cross, he answered, "That's Danner. He was right beside me when he got it just as we came ashore." They were with the first outfits ashore. So I read a prayer. The Chief Chaplain of the Mediterranean Theater, who was accompanying me, said, "Bishop, would you read a prayer here?" I looked. It was not a cross; it was a Star of David. I knelt and read the little metal tag. I think I shall never forget that boy's name: "Louis Diamond, Brooklyn, New York." It seemed to me fitting to read the Twenty-third Psalm.

Whether it comes in the moment of battle or after three score years and ten, it comes. It comes for all. Is this the end? We may wonder "for whom the bell tolls," but we know it tolls for all, rich and poor, wise and foolish, strong and weak. Some there are who warn us:

> So live, that when thy summons comes to join
> The innumerable caravan, which moves
> To that mysterious realm, where each shall take
> His chamber in the silent halls of death,
> Thou go not, like the quarry-slave at night,
> Scourged to his dungeon, but sustained and soothed
> By an unfaltering trust, approach thy grave
> Like one who wraps the drapery of his couch
> About him, and lies down to pleasant dreams.

And others stand, refusing blindfold, facing death and shouting:

> Fear death? — to feel the fog in my throat,
>   The mist in my face,
> When the snows begin, and the blasts denote
>   I am nearing the place,
> The power of the night, the press of the storm,
>   The post of the foe;
> Where he stands, the Arch Fear in a visible form,
>   Yet the strong man must go:

For the journey is done and the summit attained,
  And the barriers fall,
Though a battle's to fight ere the guerdon be
    gained,
  The reward of it all.
I was ever a fighter, so — one fight more,
  The best and the last!
I would hate that death bandaged my eyes, and
    forbore,
  And bade me creep past.
No! let me taste the whole of it, fare like my peers
  The heroes of old,
Bear the brunt, in a minute pay life's glad arrears
  Of pain, darkness and cold.
For sudden the worst turns the best to the brave,
  The black minute's at end,
And the elements' rage, the fiend-voices that rave,
  Shall dwindle, shall blend,
Shall change, shall become first a peace out of pain,
  Then a light, then thy breast,
O thou soul of my soul! I shall clasp thee again,
  And with God be the rest!

But face it as we may, it comes. The Christian tells us, "Death is swallowed up in victory." He asks, "Where, O death, is thy sting? Where, O grave, is thy victory?" He hears our Lord speak: "Let not your heart be troubled, neither let it be afraid."

Is all of this but wishful thinking? We must admit, of course, that we deal here with faith. "I believe . . . in the life everlasting." There are some who hold that there is evidence that will stand up under scientific inquiry, evidence that demonstrates life beyond the grave. A dear personal friend, of scientific and critical mind, certainly not a man to be taken in by charlatans, a man widely read, trained in a school of engineering, a world traveler who has met some of the most acute minds of our day, a man to whom a hoax is something to expose, tells me that he is completely convinced. A distinguished business-man of Jewish faith, extraordinarily able in financial matters, has reached the same conclusion. I have looked through some of the books that recount research in the realm of the psychical. I have sat in a séance and have noted the messages received. I have been impressed by the insignificant and almost irrelevant nature of the mes-sages. Surely beings to whom the future life is known would have something more significant to communicate than meaningless little repetitions of some happening of years ago. The fact, if it be a fact, that references are made by the departed to happenings known only to the dead one and the living person receiving the message may be important, but how much more important would be a message giving guidance to confused humanity from one who has conversed with the great souls of all time.

I do not speak dogmatically, not at all, but I must confess to a certain degree of agnosticism when I read the reports that come from the spiritualists or even from the Society for Psychical Research. I simply do not know. My trust is not based upon evidence. I hope that evi-dence, convincing and thus inspiring, may come. It may be here, but so far I have not seen it.

Nonetheless, I do believe in immortality. I have read

the famous Ingersoll Lectures on Immortality given from time to time at Harvard. They are stimulating. Perhaps I indulge in credulity, but believing in the fact of intelligence present and active in the universe, I cannot rest in the self-defeating conclusion that the human mind, the highest expression of creativity, is snuffed out by a physical change called death. It is to make the work of the Eternal meaningless.

Contemporary theologians talk much about the end of history. Many insist that the Kingdom of God cannot be realized in history. With human nature as it is, sinful, and of the earth, earthy, it is too much to expect, they argue, that man by his own efforts or in cooperation with the Eternal can build a society upon the earth in which God's will rules in all the activities of men. Thus the theologians speak of the great acts of God, the act of creation, the act of redemption, and finally the act of consummation. It is in this final act that history ends and a new order begins. This, to me, is highly speculative. Of course, the whole field is speculative, from one point of view. I have never been able to see why God's purpose cannot be realized in history. Whatever the fact may be — and I must say the discussion goes beyond my ability to comprehend — it seems self-evident to me that the continuing existence of life is requisite to any conception of an intelligent and moral Being called God. It is conceivable that God might repent of having created the universe, and the grotesque pictures of Gabriel blowing his horn and ending it all may have some force if we think of Deity desirous of living alone forever and forever; but for me, the Eternal Himself needs the response of love for the full satisfaction of His own personality, and such response involves other personalities. I do not like to move into such abstract areas. I simply do not know. I do know that without immortality the whole scheme of things loses its meaning for me and I, like Omar, might wish to "shatter it into bits and remold it nearer the heart's desire."

Is a flaming mind like that of Einstein or Shakespeare or Churchill, like that of St. Thomas Aquinas or Wesley, or a burning heart like that of St. Francis or Livingstone to be quenched? We pinch the wick of a candle and light is gone. Is that it? The mere fact that we crave immortality does not prove it, I know. But to question the intelligence of the Supreme Intelligence — and to me it is to question it if we see such intelligence acting like an artist who after painting a masterpiece calmly gouges the canvas or scrapes off the paint — is a matter of concern. It would appear reasonable to assume that the creativity that manifests itself in the powers of the mind, the outreaches of the soul, would carry on at least to conserve the creation for its further development. This must seem nonsense to some. It does not seem so to me. And apparently it has seemed reasonable to millions through the centuries. It is one of the cherished beliefs of humanity.

The wisest of men, the minds that have thought most deeply not only in theology but in physics and chemistry, in astronomy and biology, have held this faith. Perhaps they were mistaken. This may be all, a few brief years of struggle and of sorrow, of achievement or of failure, recognition or rejection, then a moment — the heart stops, a bullet penetrates the brain, the body is crushed in an accident. That is all! A few "mistaken" words read by a "mistaken" priest or minister, a ceremony at a grave, a stone, the loneliness of the years until my time comes! Nonsense! It is to make it all a "sorry scheme of things entire." I do not believe it. There are those who turn to the physical law of the conservation of energy and reason from that to the conservation of personality. These are all analogies, more or less impressive.

I move out in terms of the goodness of God. I have always felt inadequate when I have entered a home to which death has preceded me. Words say so little. Consolation cannot be expressed, at least not by me. I sat one day beside a great pianist. I had known her for years. Recognition had come. She had played concertos with the great symphony orchestras. Her future was secure. I had not known that cancer had come and was utterly unprepared for the change the months had wrought. The once vibrant personality was broken; agony had written its terrifying message upon her face. I wanted to say the right word. I could not find it. It hurts me to this hour; but to have spoken of death or of life, even to have repeated the great affirmations, simply would not do.

I faced it again in Italy. It was during the war. Word was brought to me when in Naples that a boy was in the stockade nearby. He belonged to my church. He had been gambling. The stakes were but five dollars. He thought he saw his opponent reach for a weapon. They had had a few drinks. His response was almost automatic. He pulled a pistol and fired. The court-martial had found him guilty of murder and had sentenced him to die. Trained to kill, he had perhaps killed before, but that was in battle. Now he must pay with his life. He had heard I was in Naples and had asked me to come. We talked for a long time. What does one say? He was self-controlled. I read from the New Testament. He seemed at peace. Then we talked of his home. I did not know he was married until he mentioned his little son. Then the poor fellow broke down. "How can you tell my mother and my boy?" His wife had deserted him. What does one say?

Just as I rose to go, he said, "Bishop, you know I have to go tomorrow morning. Would you mind coming out and standing with me?" I felt I could not do it, but said, almost machinelike, "Would it mean anything to you to have me with you?" "Yes," he replied, "it would mean a great deal to me." So at five the next morning, I was there. What does one say about immortality then? Is this all there is? Does this boy have no further chance? Was it enough that he had prayed for forgiveness? He seemed to have found solace and strength. Can a man kill and then in a few days be forgiven? And another with perhaps a deeper sense of justice feels he cannot ask God to forgive and does not. What about him? I simply do not know. I walked with that boy, and after a time he was gone. All day long that terrible scene appeared and reappeared. I could not get that boy's last words out of my mind. Then suddenly I realized that I had walked across battlefields where thousands had died, and I had taken death for granted. Jesus, it is said, had compassion on the multitude. Perhaps He thought of each one of us as I had been thinking of that boy. I think God thinks of all of us that way. I think that concern involves immortality. What the future life is like I do not know. It must be personal, at least. We must know the loved ones.

I believe that God is good, that He is a God of love. It is in His goodness, His righteousness, His love that I put my trust. And in the certainty that nothing can separate me from His love lies my hope of life everlasting.

I have lost some who are dear to me — Father, Mother, and my older brother. I am rich in the precious presence of the one who is dearer to me than life itself and in the presence of our children and grandchildren. But I know the ranks will be broken. When, who, where, I do not know. I am sure this is not all.

I want a chance to express all the love I have failed to reveal. I need eternity for that. I want to grow. So much to know, so little time!

I want to sit at the feet of the great minds of all time. The Negro sings, "I'm gonna walk all over God's heaven." I want to walk with the eager group that follows Socrates. I want to see light as Turner and Monet saw it. I want to hear Paul read the Thirteenth Chapter of First Corinthians. And perhaps Jesus would repeat the Sermon on the Mount. I need this afterchance to make the best of the present chance. When Mrs. Smith's little son is ill, desperately ill, and the family is fearful, I must put down Capek and Maxwell Anderson, Masefield and Browning, Niebuhr and Tillich — the last with a bit more ease, because I force myself through sentences and paragraphs I do not understand — I must be in Mrs. Smith's home. In the life beyond I shall listen to Tillich and watch the faces of his hearers, and if they then understand, I shall take a century or two to puzzle out the meaning — perhaps he may be revising by that time, since heaven may enlarge the thinking even of the best of our theologians.

Vachel Lindsay wrote a poem entitled "General Booth Enters Heaven." It was a dramatic portrayal of the leader of the Salvation Army marching through the gates over there with drums beating, particularly the great bass drum, the tambourines singing. I have often thought that George Fox, the Quaker, must have been much disturbed when General Booth entered heaven. Fox was a man who had penetrated the silences and had understood the full meaning of the command, "Be still and know that I am God." I am sure that General Booth long since has sat in silence in one of Fox's meetings and learned to wait until the Spirit moved him. No doubt he has risen from his knees with new "concern" in his heart. I would not be a bit surprised that Fox too, having met General Booth, has stood on one of the golden streets with the Salvation Army band and has heard the beating of the drums and perhaps himself has taken a tambourine and has shared in the taking of the collection at General Booth's command. We need eternity to learn from each other so that we may know indeed.

I need immortality to be mortal in the truest sense. I must live forever to live at all. I think there is justification for the faith in immortality because of the life that emerges from the faith. Just as I judge Hinduism by the dulling of the social conscience that is the inevitable accompaniment of the doctrine of transmigration, so too do I judge faith in the life everlasting. The Hindu beholds a man suffering. He may decide that the man in his suffering is but doing proper penance and making proper payment for the sinning in a previous life. To be sympathetic is to interfere with the process of divine justice. Therefore, to lighten his load may be immoral. For a Christian, to relieve suffering is to serve Christ and thereby be ready for immortality.

The man who knows he is to live forever differs from the man who cries, "Eat, drink, and be merry, for tomorrow we die." If this is all, the sensual makes heavy claim. If there is no future to face, if there be no judgment, if I am to enter eternity with so much to make up before I can get on the way, I live differently. It is not a matter of fear. It is but a calm consideration of facts as they are. If I know that my Redeemer liveth and that I too shall live; if the abiding forces are faith, hope, and love; if the fruits of the spirit are love and joy and peace; if the "Well done" that I am to hear is related to the cup of cold water, the turning of a key in a prison door, to food and clothing, I get a new sense of values.

I learn there is only so much food I can eat, only so many suits I can wear, only so much of the physical before satiety sets in, but in the realm of the true, the good, and the beautiful there are no limits. I turn, therefore, to the Bread of Life and to the Waters of the Spirit.

I do not act because of reward, or because of fear, but because I am to live with myself forever, the kind of self I am developing. If I die soon and that is all, what of it? But if the acts, added up, mean me, if I must be like that through the years, until eternity does its transforming work in me, then immortality, like the tug of the moon upon the tides, pulls me.

I saw a sad procession in a village outside Manila. Two men were carrying a little silver-painted casket, one on either side of it, followed by a young woman whose face was hidden by a black veil, and behind them friends. Many carried flowers. They were walking in silence to a little plot of ground. Is the smile of a little child, its gleeful shout and its response to a mother, a father, to be no more? Or are they to see that baby again? I have no proof. I do not need it. This something my soul demands. It must be true. In any case, I believe it so deeply that I live upon its sustaining strength. Jesus believed it. Paul believed it. The Church has believed it. Holy Scripture affirms it.

"I believe . . . in the life everlasting."

In the deeply moving correspondence that passed between George Bernard Shaw and the Abbess of Stanbrook, published in the *Atlantic* under the fascinating title "The Nun and the Dramatist," Shaw refers to a Palestinian trip and a request that the Abbess had made that he bring back a relic from Calvary. Shaw approaches much of Palestine reverently, but is revolted by the base commercialization of sacred spots that the money-mad have associated with Jesus. Shaw knew that the place where the crosses stood was unknown, and therefore sought the relic not at Calvary but in Bethlehem. From the threshold of the Church of the Nativity, he picked up "a scrap of the limestone rock which certainly existed when the feet of Jesus pattered about on it and the feet of Mary pursued him to keep him in order." He tells us that he picked up two stones, "one to be thrown blind-fold among the others in Stanbrook garden so that there may always be a stone from Bethlehem there, though nobody will know which it is and be tempted to steal it . . ." And then he said the other stone was for the Abbess herself. He writes that he will bring these stones, "unless I perish on the way, in which case I shall present myself at the heavenly gate with a stone in each hand, and St. Peter will stand at attention and salute the stones (incidentally saluting ME) when he has unlocked the gate and flung it open before me. At least he would if it were ever locked, which I don't believe."

I think Mr. Shaw was right, the doors are not locked. The whole question of rewards and punishments is a difficult one. Is the immortality announced in the affirmation, "I believe . . . in the life everlasting," to be for but a few, or is it to be an immortality of bliss for some and punishment for others? Is the brief span of years that we call life to determine the status of every individual for all eternity?

For many years, I was associated with court and prison as boys, so glibly designated as delinquents, were taken before the authorities. I know that society must be protected from the antisocial, from the predatory, the beastly. But I found it hard to understand the term "justice." In one state a man might receive twenty years for a crime that across the line in another state would be punished by a sentence of but ten years. In some courts where the judge was "tough" long sentences were meted out; in another, moderate sentences, all in the name of "justice"! We, of course, are limited by the frailties of humanity. In the case of the All Wise, the All Loving, what then? What is absolute justice?

I know men who have worked it out, apparently to their own satisfaction. Sin demands payment. Yesterday, many offenses called for capital punishment. Today, we move away from the death penalty. Neat formulas appear right to the legalistic mind. The pound of flesh may be the payment, but to pay it is to die. The sins of a short life are to be paid by an eternity of torment.

I don't know much about heaven and hell. The New Testament test which indicated, "Inasmuch as ye have done it unto one of the least of these, ye have done it unto Me" and which appears to find the reasons for eternal life to lie in the giving of a cup of cold water, feeding the hungry, and visiting those who are in prison, will, I fear, keep many a prelate out of heaven and admit many a doubter.

I recall a situation in Los Angeles. A young mother, deserted, lonely, but determined to care for her little girl, sought work. She had no training. When I met her, she was dancing in a cheap dance hall on Fourth Street. There were ten or twenty girls there. The patrons of the hall would buy tickets and could dance with any girl of their choice. The dances were brief, the earnings were small. The answer was "dates." And so she supported her child. She was with the little one through most of the day, danced from eight until twelve, and got home after "overtime." Uneducated, yes; but strangely enough there was refinement in her speech, and she read much. What was she? A prostitute? A dancer? A mother? She had made no profession of religion, but she loved that child, hated her "work," and dreamed of the day when it would be different.

Another young mother lived in the same city. She had inherited wealth. She was a member of the church. She had a son. Selfishly, she left him to the care of a maid, and she made the rounds of social life. She took out more than she put in. A parasite? Her conversation was small talk, the repetition of rumor, the recitation of class prejudice. Respectable. She said, "Lord, Lord."

I do not judge these women. Certainly I do not condone conduct that debases. But at the judgment seat who says, "Hell for you," and, "Heaven for you," and to which of these women are the words spoken?

I know decision here it not easy. Years ago, I received a telegram from a father. His son was in prison in Los Angeles. I went to see the boy. The guard who admitted me to the cell whispered, "Watch your step; this one is high power." He was charged with six counts of highway robbery, and was guilty. The district attorney, who later went to San Quentin himself, was out to make a record. I got the boy an attorney. Finally, an agreement was reached that he would plead guilty to two counts and would not be prosecuted for six. But each count carried a penalty of five years to life. Years later, he was paroled to me. He had a keen mind, ability to write, an artistic temperament, and a good deal of personal charm. He went to New York. He decided to sail the Caribbean and to write a book. Sailing boats are not secured without money. So the young man who had been in prison and apparently had learned nothing went to an arms store and asked to see a pistol. "Do you have ammunition to fit this gun?" he asked. The ammunition was brought, and he loaded the pistol and held up the salesman. With the money in his pockets, he rushed to the street, hailed a taxi, and ordered the driver to get out of that section in a hurry. The driver was a man of nerve, and yelled to a traffic policeman that he had a bandit in the car. The policeman's whistle summoned other policemen. The young man jumped out of the taxicab, shot at the officers, but fortunately hit no one, and was finally captured. Then followed Sing Sing and Dannemora. When at last he was released, authorities from three states claimed him. He was returned to California, and served the rest of his sentence. Then came the war and apparent rehabilitation. He worked on the Alaskan highway, and finally opened a business in San

Francisco. A few more clashes with the law, and at last news of his death in Brazil, the circumstances of which I need not recite. What about him? He broke his father's heart, and betrayed every effort I had made. He was dangerous. The answer here was not too difficult — jail and more jail — if such be an answer. What about eternity? I don't know. I have known of men whose conduct was close to criminal, brutal at home, and then a brain operation followed and a new man emerged from the operating room. Now they tell me that conduct can be determined by blood composition, certain balances in a criminal, other balances in a saint. What about responsibility? The loaf of bread is stolen, and Jean Valjean goes to the hulks. In the terrible history of the slave trade, fifteen million Africans were torn from their homes and the slave ships sailed the seas. Or, again, a continent is stolen. A new morality comes, the slave trade is gone, but questions are still raised in Angola, and a church cooperates with a state, both of which deny that slavery exists; it is not slavery, it is contract, they say, forced, yes, but contractual nevertheless. All of this must be worked out, and I believe it can be; but those who sit in judgment seem to forget that our Blessed Lord Himself said, "Judge not that ye be not judged."

What about a Hitler? No hell, you say? Then there is but one answer: the universe is an insane asylum. I have stood before the piles of naked bodies at Buchenwald. They lay like cordwood before the crematories — in Germany, hundreds of thousands of Jews dead! No hell? Then no justice.

Should the answer be oblivion? Do we have the freedom to forfeit eternity? When does the second chance become the last chance? I do not know. I believe in the life everlasting. I believe God is love as well as justice. I trust Him. I am sure there is an answer in His infinite wisdom. But I cannot believe God's love closes the door to redeemability. When a man comes to himself, I believe the Father will be waiting for him, ready to place a ring upon his finger, robes upon his body. The son who was lost is found again. Does the time come, however, when the privilege of forgiveness has been exhausted, the die cast and forever?

There is a hell. Have we not lived in it? Remorse, regret! The brutal word, the selfish deed, the immoral act! Memory is both blessing and curse. There is not only the power of a great memory, but the evil act lives on, never to be forgotten. What we do lives. A great pitcher was urged to throw an occasional bean ball, to brush the batter back from the plate. Said the tempter, "Nobody will know you did it deliberately." "You are wrong," the pitcher answered. "I would know." We know, and always.

It is right here that so much of our bad mental health develops. The weight of wrong breaks our backs. We must have help, forgiveness. And with Him there is plenteous redemption. God's love is unfailing, we say. Does it cease to operate when I become the new being that follows death? Is God's love toward me but the ephemeral interest that a man might have in a mosquito that is here an hour or two and gone? Surely not.

This is no letting down of the bars, no declaration of "Eat, drink, and be merry, for tomorrow you have another shot at whatever it is." Not at all! "To be alone with my conscience is hell enough for me," said Edgar Allan Poe. It is. There is punishment, self-inflicted, the punishment that flows from the broken law, more than physical, much, much to pay. But I am talking about life everlasting. Surely a God who sent His Son out of love continues to be the seeking God who forever seeks the lost coin, the lost sheep, the lost son.

Heaven must be that state in which the seeking soul finds absolute joy in the love of the Eternal and in doing His will. Not nirvana, not the end of desire, not the loss of personality; on the contrary, new and consuming desire, the desire to do His will; life abundant, the full development of the personality until the person takes on divinity.

He said, "I go to prepare a place for you . . . that where I am, there ye may be also." Someone has put it beautifully: We are guests of God. That is enough for me! To be with such a one as Christ, that is enough. It does not mean separation. He loved people, little children, men and women. The place He would prepare must conserve all the richest joys of life at its best, the best here — in a word, love. The place must include the spirit that was manifest to the woman taken in adultery, to the rich young ruler, to Zaccheus, to Peter who denied Him and to Thomas who doubted Him, and, yes, even to Judas who betrayed Him. At the very end, there in the Garden, Jesus called Judas "friend." And greater love hath no man than this, that he lay down his life for his friend.

I think that is the spirit that is over there. Perhaps I am wrong. Perhaps it is a judge with heart hardened who damns forever — but what is the crime? Unbelief? Ignorance? Sins of the flesh? Greed? Where is perfection? Does it lie in creedal correctness? Is it a matter of acceptance of faith upon authority? Are we to be rewarded because we raise no questions?

I wish I could find satisfaction in the jargon of the scribes and the Pharisees, the doctors and the saints. I wish I could be honest and at the same time accept the dogmatic statements that the untutored repeat with such passion. They sit in judgment upon so many. They damn the publicans and sinners, and speak of the apostate. It was Jesus Himself who said, "Call no man good." We must approach all these issues in the humility that is born of love.

I quoted Omar at the beginning of this chapter. He said that he when young had frequented doctor and saint and "heard great argument about it and about," but evermore came out by the same door wherein he went. I, too, have heard great argument, but have not come out by the same door wherein I went. I have stood in the presence of One who is far beyond doctor and saint. I do not hear argument upon His lips. I do hear Him say, "He that hath seen Me hath seen the Father." In seeing Him and learning that the Father is like Him, I bow in simple trust. I can't answer the man who asks, "You admit that you are to be a witness?" except to say, "Yes." I know he has the right to ask the question, but what is it you witness to? "Put it down. Say it. Define it. Unless you can state the faith clearly, you cannot witness. In fact, you do not have it unless you can state it." But is that so? I can't define my love for my wife, my children, my parents. I cannot put down my love for country. How can I tell a man from another land what America means to me? It would sound boastful to him. But when I return from abroad and I see the banner flying, the waves breaking upon these dear shores, the mountains towering against the skies; when I think of Jefferson and of Lincoln, of free schools and free platforms and a free press, and I dream of "alabaster cities undimmed by human tears" — what is it, this faith in democracy, this love of country? Yes, define it! I must try. When I consider life eternal and think of God and of creation, I simply cannot set it down.

Masefield in "Dauber" tells of a boy who would paint. "I cannot get it — not yet," he said:

> That leap and light and sudden change to green
> And all the glittering from the sunset's red,
> And the milky colors where the bursts have been,
> And then the clipper striding like a queen . . .

Yes, try to put that down in the terminology of the legalist. Jesus does it all so much better in His parables. There we read the words that lived in His person — the second mile, the cup of cold water, the petition, "Give us this day our daily bread." Forgive seventy times seven, yes, but that meant millions, a number unlimited.

So when He says, "Let not your heart be troubled; ye

believe in God, believe also in Me," I do. When He says quietly, "In my Father's house are many mansions; I go to prepare a place for you," I am not interested in the size of the rooms or the style of architecture. Knowing Him as I do, I simply turn to the One He revealed and say with Browning, "I trust what Thou shalt do."

Perhaps the day will come when all this can be put down in a book: "HEAVEN — see page 4765." Read the definition, the final word; cease to ponder, it is down at last. I don't think so. Someday we may pierce the curtain, not an iron one but the veil that at present is mystery. We may know as we are known. Faith does last on; so, too, hope. But the greatest of these is love. It is in that love that I face the future, all of it, unafraid.

"I believe . . . in the life everlasting."

CHAPTER IV

I Believe in Prayer

MY MOTHER taught me to pray. At first I repeated the simple prayers of childhood: "Now I lay me down to sleep," "Gentle Jesus, meek and mild." I learned the Lord's Prayer and repeated it at church. I do not now recall what these prayers meant to me.

My father was gifted in speech, and prayed in the tradition of the people called Methodists. Methodist prayer was clothed in the dignified diction of the King James Version of the Bible, and in the reverent language of Charles Wesley's hymns. Again and again my father's public prayers began with Isaac Watts's majestic salutation, "O God, our help in ages past, Our hope for years to come." For a long period there was family prayer in our home.

Prayer was natural, personal, helpful. I never questioned its validity. I assumed there was a Father to whom we could go, a Father who heard and cared and who answered prayer. Problems arose later. Did prayer change God's will? Was prayer impertinent? I knew that Jesus had taught us to pray. I also knew that many of His prayers were unanswered. What did it mean?

Later, I read Harry Emerson Fosdick's *The Meaning of Prayer*. It was helpful because it was honest, scholarly, devout. Then came association with the churches which have preserved the great prayers of Christian liturgy. I have been deeply moved when repeating the petitions of the Prayer Book, and have shared in such prayers at Canterbury, at Lambeth Palace and Westminster Abbey, and also in Trinity Church, Boston, where the worshiper can almost hear the voice of Phillips Brooks leading the people in prayer. Prayers at Thessalonica, where my dear friend Metropolitan Panteleimon presided at the solemn and sacred service according to the Holy Liturgy of the Greek Orthodox Church, were an experience of sheer ecstasy, as were the prayers at the funeral service of Archbishop Germanos in London. But what does it all mean?

We do not live by logic. Who approaches the girl he loves with a logically formulated proposal for marriage? Not a man who is in love! A racketeer seeking to seduce a wealthy and foolish widow might. His purpose is to steal a fortune from a poor old lady who is captivated by his pretty compliments and infatuated by his simulated passion. His plan of conquest may be carefully conceived. But the true lover does not approach his beloved that way.

There is truth that appears to evade syllogisms. I would not discount logic. We must think straight and syllogisms are proper. A night sky full of stars, the sea in storm, midnight on the desert, or the forest at dawn — what happens to the rhapsodic response and the warm heart when such experiences are put down in the cold, descriptive terms of scientific record? Rapture refuses the embrace of logic. The soul will not be shackled. But, ought not a man to be coldly rational when choosing a lifetime mate? Surely scientific data must be present for eugenic decision. Such data no doubt have their place, but a man in love rushes to his loved one to say, "I love you." Is it to be thought irrational to turn to the Creator in love and respect?

The heart possesses knowledge denied the brain. I know the heart does not reason. It is an important muscle, but it is not the center of knowledge. Why not talk sense? I am. When I discount logic or the scientific method, a sense of shame steals over me at first; in fact, I feel a certain loss of self-respect. I am intellectually pledged to the scientific method, but there are areas in which truth is apprehended by other means. There is a world not conquered by questionnaires. It is apprehended by intuition. Poets and artists know this; in fact, much of the truly creative in scientific advance has come from the great leaps of faith into the unknown by men of science whose minds were ready for new generalization.

A young lady of twenty stood by a teacher's desk in a church school classroom. The soft light from the stained-glass windows illuminated her lovely face — I knew it was she, and no one else. And it was. True enough, the psychologist may have his explanation — the lure of glorious black hair, eyes full of light, the high color of healthy cheeks — but all his data fail to explain. There were certainty, joy, wonder — yes, reverence. I cannot put it down, but I knew then that I loved her, and the years have validated the truth of that assurance.

So too with prayer. I am as certain of God's love as I am of the undying affection of my beloved. I cannot prove either conclusion. I know. The Lord is my Shepherd; He cares for me. "In the beginning God . . ." He created me. "He causes the sun to shine upon the just and the unjust . . ." He sustains the universe. "God is a refuge . . ." He is always there. Of course, I can understand the scholar who insists that prayer does not change God one iota, that it does not affect his conduct or alter natural law. That is a logical inference based upon ivory-tower contemplation of the attributes of Deity. If He be all-knowing, all-powerful, everywhere present, if it be that He has a purpose He is going to realize in the earth, then logically it would appear that our little petitions are like the whimpering of a baby that does not turn a wise mother from a proper course in rearing a little one. But is this really true?

I know prayer changes me. I become a different person and thus a changed factor in God's plans. In one case he cannot use me, in another he can.

Is prayer but autosuggestion given another name by clever or scheming clerics? It is no answer, I know, to say that Jesus prayed. But He did, and the man who

knew more about God than any man who has lived, a
man who had mastered the laws of the spiritual life and
stood in the presence of the Eternal as "beloved Son,"
summoned us to our knees, not in the market place
for a pretense but in the quiet of the closed room. I
think His call is entitled to serious consideration. The
fact that He prayed is of importance to me. I am impressed by the fact that throughout history man has
stood in the presence of a power greater than himself
and has sought to reach the mind of God.

When in the Garden of Gethsemane Jesus cried, "May
this cup pass from me," it was the appeal of a son to a
father. Jesus apparently believed that the Father could
save Him from the Cross, and would do so if He thought
best. Of course, Jesus added, "But not my will, Thy will
be done." This attitude is basic in any approach to God.
This is an expression of the honest desire that all decisions shall be in accord with God's will. Prayer creates
the mood in which the individual can be used most ef-
fectively to reveal God's will.

Prayer is first of all an affirmation of faith in God. God
is a personality who knows me so well that the hairs of my
head are numbered. He loves me so completely that
even with a universe to sustain, law to maintain, and
plans to provide for the unending succession of sunrises and the consistent coming of night after night, I
am in His thought and affection. The God who carries
in His mind the whirling spheres and the unfolding
flowers knows me. This is the faith upon which prayer
is based. I cannot pray unless I believe.

Prayer is more than affirmation of theism. It is encounter. The Eternal who is being sought by me is ever seeking me. We meet in prayer. It is like meeting a friend upon a busy thoroughfare. Thousands are rushing by. They do not know my name, but my friend does. There is the flash of recognition, the word of greeting. I count in the crowd. I am an individual known and knowing. Prayer is like that. I can meet Him in crowded street, in quiet garden, in the soft lights of the chapel. Trysts at twilight transform encounter into enchanted evening.

In such encounter I learn to know God better. I discover His will. I resolve to put myself at His disposal in a new and dedicated sense. Not my will, but Thine be done. When I pray for others, I bring them into this encounter. I think of them in a new light, because we stand together in the presence of God. We are together before the throne. I see them as persons who are loved by God and I learn more fully that in His sight they are beings of infinite worth. I think, too, of others who are praying for me. They are encountering God. When I repeat the Creed and say, "I believe in . . . the communion of saints," I recall that fellow Christians have communed with God and have brought my name to the Father in prayer. We say we have fellowship with one another and with Him. We do. Prayer changes things. Others say, not so. I know it changes me, and I believe that when we pray together or even separately, prayer changes all who so participate.

Jesus taught us to pray and in so doing put his stamp

of approval upon the practice of prayer. He indicated the attitude of mind and heart requisite to prayer. He said, "When ye pray, say: Our Father . . ." This is first an affirmation of faith, but it is more. He said, "Hallowed be thy name." The approach is one of reverence. This rules out much of the mechanical associated with much prayer. Prayer can never be fully significant when it is but the repetition of petition which was once meaningful but has now become little more than the routine telling of beads, or the endeavor to appease a Being whom we fear. Is there a conflict between teaching a child to pray, with the resultant habitual performance of an act, and the actual experience of God's love in the moment of adoration and of dedication?

I am fearful of mechanics. Some Buddhists have their prayer wheels. A prayer is written upon a bit of paper or parchment and placed in a cylinder on a short stick. The cylinder is spun and spun and the prayer is thought to be offered at each turn, and thus ascends and ascends. Now that recordings can be made, and electronic devices are at hand, prayer of this type can be offered continuously and mechanically. This is what prayer is not. Prayer involves persons in communion. What woman would appreciate loud-speakers in every room of the house and the recorded word of love from a husband at a ball game. No, it is the embrace at the door when the husband returns home or the understanding but silent conveying of love in the flash of the eye, the smile upon the face. It must be personal.

I recall a devout Christian friend who knelt each morn-

ing by his bed. He had a stack of three-by-five cards before him. On each card was the name of a person. He
remembered each one in prayer each day. I think he
had as many as a hundred cards. The idea back of this
was sincere, perhaps even sound. But the prayer period
became increasingly a procedure, artificial, almost mechanical. And there was a certain degree of unfortunate
pride in the later announcement, "I remembered one
hundred in prayer this morning." I do not criticize, nor
do I discount this method. But how far do we go in this
filing-system approach to God? If Jesus is correct, the
Father knoweth our needs before we ask. I watch men
bow to say grace in a crowded restaurant, or in the din-
ing car. I cannot do that without a sense of parade.
Perhaps I should witness in this fashion to my faith in
God and my gratitude for food, but I cannot. I do not
criticize the Mohammedan who places his prayer mat
on the earth or floor, wherever he may be, and at stated
intervals prays toward Mecca. In fact, I respect him. No
doubt I might win respect too if I were equally faithful, but I cannot, or at least do not. It is like praying
on the street corner with a loud voice. Jesus condemned
that, or at least the spirit that lay back of it. I find the
appeal to privacy, the summons to the secret prayer
room, more congenial.

There are those who impress me as lecturing the Holy
One when they are engaged in prayer. Some prayers
are like a presumptuous young Freshman who seeks to
instruct a famous scholar. But why should we commune
with Him at all? There is nothing He does not know.

Yes, God is all-knowing. And a grandfather knows so much more than the trusting little granddaughter whose baby finger points out the bluebird. I love her and her joyful gesture is interesting and inspiring to me. Not that her comment, "See the birdie, Granddaddy," is a substitute for Maeterlinck or Audubon, but I love to be in communion with her little mind and rejoice in the tiny hand that grasps my finger when we walk in the woods. Her words are significant to me. I believe God cares too. When I reach up a hand in prayer, I know a hand is reached down to me.

Like an athlete, the man who would pray must train. He must keep in condition. There are people who would do well to hang up a sign often seen in a factory or in transportation: TO BE USED ONLY IN CASE OF EMERGENCY. Prayer is for emergency use, something thought to be available in crisis. Such prayer is almost sacrilegious. Occasionally an athlete of a generation gone will attempt today to throw a baseball or punt a football. Usually the attempt is a dismal performance. Men who pray only when the ship is sinking or the aircraft is on fire can expect little to happen to themselves or to the situation.

Prayer properly begins at a mother's knee. It is a case of learning by doing. The child prays and in the act unconsciously affirms the fact of God. He learns to thank God for the beauty of the earth, the beauty of the skies. It is God's world in which he lives; it is upon God he relies for morning sun, for gentle breezes, refreshing showers. When God finished the work of creation, He saw that it was good. So, too, a child, when from prayer he turns to God's good world. But a thoughtful child will wonder about tornado and drought, earthquake and fire. He may demand some justification of God's ways to men, long before he hears of Milton and *Paradise Lost*. A way to truth lies in the practice of prayer, and fuller understanding of God is found as the way is traversed. Prayer must be continuous, that is, a daily practice. It is the cessation of prayer that destroys the values that lie in prayer. Just as muscles atrophy and the athlete of yesterday is the pitiful figure of today, if he has failed to keep fit, so, too, the devout moments of childhood are lost to youth if he long since has ceased to pray.

Prayer must be continuous. Like breathing, it is essential to life itself. When the *Titanic* struck the iceberg, men and women reacted differently, some courageously, some cowardly. A prayer born of fear is not likely to strengthen the individual who possesses none of the strength that a life of prayer develops. True enough, "Nearer, my God, to Thee" was played by the ship's orchestra and no doubt sung by many facing death. But why should God be nearer at such a moment than at every moment? The practice of prayer keeps the person in daily contact with God. He is always near.

Thus, the great religious personalities have urged prayer at regular intervals, Morning Prayer, Evening Prayer.

Prayer assumes the fact of God. It assumes the Eternal is not only always there, but is actively seeking each person so that His will may be known. God is good. There is a word that carries the full concept of good-

ness and more. That word is "holy." When at the beginning of the day we respond to the seeking God, it is
natural that our own mood should determine the nature
of our response. There are days when our first desire is
to confess our sins. All of us come short of the glory of
God. Yesterday was far from a proper expression of
Christian love on our part. We pray for forgiveness, we
confess. Sometimes we speak out of our own limited
vocabularies; sometimes we repeat the great prayers of
confession of the Church: "Almighty and most merciful
Father, we have erred and strayed from Thy ways like
lost sheep. We have followed too much the devices and
desires of our own hearts. We have offended against
Thy holy laws. We have left undone those things which
we ought to have done . . ." And properly, as in the
great prayer, we pray "that we may hereafter live a
godly, righteous, and sober life." Yes, and "to the glory
of Thy holy Name." There are other mornings, not in
any sense of self-righteousness, that we lift up our hearts,
not in confession, but in adoration. In the *Adoramus
Te* we sing, "We do adore Thee, O Christ, and magnify
Thy holy name." It is this adoration that well nigh over-
whelms us when we come into the presence of God.
Adoration becomes praise, and praise becomes thanksgiving. When in such a mood we meet the morning,
light itself is joy, light that brings color to the fields,
the hills, the waters of the nearby lake. The birds sing
as night skies become the skies of dawn. We join with
Henry van Dyke and say, "Joyful, joyful, we adore
Thee, God of glory, Lord of love; Hearts unfold like

flowers before Thee, Opening to the sun above. . . .
Giver of immortal gladness, Fill us with the light of day!"
Or we sing with Reginald Heber, "Holy, holy, holy! Lord
God Almighty! Early in the morning our song shall rise to
Thee." We praise Him: "Only Thou art holy; there is
none beside Thee, Perfect in power, in love, and
purity." We are in the presence of God, whether the
prayer be one of confession, or of adoration, praise,
thanksgiving. Perhaps we begin the day with the sustaining certainty of God's care; in a word, with assurance.
I know the sun will shine and the stars keep their courses.
I know too that "I cannot drift beyond His love and
care." I have mentioned these reactions to God at early
morning simply to stress the fact that a man who has
begun each day for twenty years in this fashion differs
from the man who has separated himself from God
either thoughtlessly or deliberately, or through doubt. A
crisis comes. The man who has prayed knows this is our
Father's world. He knows nothing can separate him from
the love of God. He brings to the moment of decision
the strength of assurance. It makes no difference whether
it be high honor with its subtle temptation of pride and
undue self-esteem, or the sinking deck of a great ocean
liner in disaster, he is with God. The man who in des-
peration cries out to a Being he does not know, from a
soul untrained for sorrow or suffering or death, will be
heard — God always hears — but is unready.

John Porter is a pseudonym. The true name is Robert
Guy McCutchan, former dean of the School of Music at
DePauw University, the editor of the Methodist Hymnal,

musician and composer extraordinary. He took George
Herbert's lovely verse and set the words to music that is
at once reverent adoration and rapturous praise. The
man of prayer can sing them.

> Let all the world in every corner sing:
> My God and King!
> The heavens are not too high,
> His praise may thither fly;
> The earth is not too low,
> His praises there may grow.
> Let all the world in every corner sing;
> My God and King!

Most of our prayers in the Christian community end
with the words "for Jesus Christ's sake" or "through
Jesus Christ our Lord." When the day is begun with
prayer, when confession is made and praise is voiced,
there comes a sense of obligation. Prayer is in Jesus'
name. He taught us to pray and He taught us much
more. There is a Father. There are also brothers. The
day begins in the presence of God. It is lived not only
in God's presence but in the presence of our brothers.
No man can rise from prayer to exploit his brother.
There is a social aspect of prayer sometimes overlooked.
I do not speak here of corporate worship where we pray
together. I speak rather of social obligation. It is our
Father's world, and sons committed to Christ are obligated not only to live in love and charity with their
neighbors, but to build a society in which social practice
expresses love and the attitude toward brother is one
that emerges from charity.

This prayer may eventuate in petition and interces-
sion. We pray for each other, not as mechanical routine,
but as men who love each other.

Morning prayer is not enough. It gets the day off to a
good start. In the home, "Grace Before Meals" is an expression of thanksgiving, the expressed recognition of
God's blessings, but it is more. There is a binding
quality about the act. When I bow and say, "We thank
Thee for these blessings," I know that in every land,
in millions of homes, the family bows similarly at meal-
time. I am bound to such brothers whether they be in
China or Russia or in the "free world."

Prayer sounds the death knell of totalitarian tyranny.
No state is really totalitarian as long as there are those
who hold there is a power greater than the state, and
this is done whenever grace is said. The cross may not be
visible, or it may still surmount the spire or stand in
sacred beauty upon the altar, but visible or invisible, it
is present in the hearts of those who pray. Even in the
darkest days of tyranny, the cross "towers o'er the wrecks
of time." When the swastika and the hammer and sickle
are but reminders of historical nightmare, the cross will
live on in the power of an endless life.

There are men who go apart for a few minutes each
day to pray — some to a downtown chapel, some to an
office window where the sky is visible, and some pray
while standing before a machine. The place is not important; the practice is. There is a renewal of faith in the
Creator and Sustainer whom we revere, a deepening understanding of the Father whom we adore. The individ-

ual knows he is working in harmony with the nature of things. Jesus said, "My Father worketh hitherto and I work." We are exalted and become consciously fellow workers with God.

Next to early morning prayer, prayer before sleep is most helpful. In prayer there is therapeutic cleansing of the soul, the freeing of the self from fear, hatred, and worry. There may be physical reasons why sleep eludes us, and a physician's care may be indicated, but large numbers of men and women would find rest and early sleep if they lay down at night following a period of prayer.

Sometimes prayer requires no words. It is but the opening of the windows of the heart to the cleansing winds of heaven. Generally, prayer should be phrased. The mind is apt to wander. Hence, the great collections of prayers. A little volume like *Great Souls at Prayer,* edited by Mary R. Tileston, or *Anthologies of Prayer,* edited by A. S. T. Fisher, will prove helpful. *The Prayer Book* and other Books of Worship should be available.

Saint Francis prayed:

O Lord, our Christ, may we have Thy mind and Thy spirit. Make us instruments of Thy peace; where there is hatred, let us sow love; where there is injury, pardon; where there is discord, union; where there is doubt, faith; where there is despair, hope; where there is darkness, light; and where there is sadness, joy.

O divine Master, grant that we may not so much seek to be consoled, as to console; to be understood, as to understand; to be loved, as to love; for it is in giving that we receive; it is in pardoning that we are pardoned; and it is in dying that we are born to eternal life. Amen.

As I consider the petitions of his prayer I find myself entering a new fellowship. I have come to know Saint Francis. So, too, other saints of history. It strengthens me to know that throughout the centuries men and women have stood or knelt to pray. Some were gifted in speech and their prayers are full of beauty. In some there is the rhythm of song and verse, and my heart beats in rhythmic response. Sincerity, or its lack, is easily discerned. When prayer is contrived for pleasing effect, it becomes a living contradiction. Prayers may be carefully written, but the prayer that moves is the prayer that comes from a heart already moved by the love of God. Prayer is not a literary exercise, it is the voicing of gratitude, the singing of praise, the cry for forgiveness, the affirmation of reverence and of adoration, the pledging of all to One who is All in All.

Whether at morning or evening prayer, or in the prayer at midday, prayer should be petition for guidance. The answer may call for a course other than the one contemplated. Not that a voice from the heavens calls out, "Do this," or, "Do not do this," but that the worshiper who seeks earnestly to know God's will often finds himself better understanding his obligations to God and to brother, and realizes the wisdom of another course.

In the City Road Chapel, built by John Wesley in London, a simple form of prayer is recommended to all:

It is advisable to fix definite times for prayer, and to guard those times for this high purpose. The best times are the early morning and the late evening, but we can pray at all times.

Allow sufficient time for time not to matter. We cannot pray with our eye on the clock.

In prayer our first thought should be of God. A good way to start to pray is to ponder over a hymn or psalm.

What God has to say to us is much more important than what we say to Him; so our prayers should include Bible reading and meditation.

Tell God every detail of your needs in earnest and thankful prayer. Thanksgiving is often the key to prayer: do not forget to say thanks. You can pray for anything you like, but expect to find God altering your likes and dislikes, for the aim of prayer is not to get what we want but to become what God wants.

This will often lead us to realise we have made mistakes and are in the wrong, but never forget that as soon as we are sufficiently sorry to want to turn from the wrong God forgives it and helps us.

Prayer is encounter; it is also enrichment. It is the testimony of great souls who have learned to pray that the practice enriches life. Such persons have learned that prayer is not begging. It is fellowship. "Blessed are the pure in heart, for they shall see God." Prayer validates the truth of the Beatitude. The sincere soul dare not approach God in impurity. The pure see Him, the impure are blinded. There can be no mental reservations, no hidden life, no refusal to confess sin, when a man kneels before God. Life is enriched by prayer because in prayer the individual with conscious effort separates himself from the degrading effects of the lie, the double standard, and even the sin that temporarily satisfies. Enrichment, however, is less a matter of what we discard than of what we appropriate. We sing, "Lord, speak to me that I may speak . . . teach that I may teach." When the mind is open to the enlightenment, the love, and the summons of God, prayer is like the ineffable moments of a symphony with Toscanini, or the unspeakable satisfaction that suffuses the soul when standing before a Rembrandt portrait, an exquisite Vermeer, the light of Monet.

In prayer the mind and heart are made ready for the mind of God. Prayer is spiritual intercourse. Prayer is communication. Truth so communicated does make us free. It is quite impossible to reach the heart of God if the kneeling suppliant carries hatred for brother in his own heart. Jesus made that clear. The God who gave His only begotten Son for our salvation is not likely to be reached in prayer by a man whose life is full of greed. Debauchery is no prelude to devotion. Like the shoes of the street that must be left at the door when a visitor enters a Japanese home, so too the shoes of enmity, selfishness, and sensuality must be removed before we enter the closet to pray.

Prayer is commitment. "Come clean," we say to the accused who sits at an interrogation table in the police station. "Come clean" is a proper order when we pray. But when we "come clean," something happens. "When I survey the wondrous cross," we sing. There is but one result: "Love so amazing, so divine, demands my soul, my life, my all."

In prayer we survey the revelation of God. Perhaps the mind may center upon the righteousness of God. Human righteousness appears always limited; in prayer we behold the absolute righteousness of One whose very nature makes it impossible for Him to do wrong. No life is ever quite the same after periods of prayer in which we confront a Being who is at once absolutely just and of such love that He stands ever ready to forgive. Or again, if prayer becomes contemplation in the presence of God, and the wonders of the universe are considered, prayer illuminates. Experiences that enkindle seldom come to those whose prayer is sporadic. Here as everywhere practice that becomes habit is essential. The values of worship are not to be discovered by attending church once a year on Easter Sunday. An occasional visit to an art gallery does not open doors to the unprepared. Rome reveals little to the Baedeker-carrying, wrist-watch tourist with an American Express itinerary before his eyes. Prayer takes time. As in travel what is brought to the scene determines what is seen, so in prayer those who have eyes to see and ears to hear are enriched.

Prayer strengthens, not every time but cumulatively.

We move from strength to strength. The courage so often revealed by men who have faced the mob, dared gibbet, and victoriously withstood brainwashing is a courage born of prayer. Such men know they work with God. They know that nothing can separate them from the love of God. They are strong in the Lord. When they walk in the valley of the shadow of death, they fear no evil. They declare, "Thou art with me. I shall dwell in the house of the Lord forever." In the last moment there is strength to cry, "Into Thy hands I commend my spirit."

Prayer is personal. There is no question about that. It is based upon the assumption that there is a Supreme Being who is at least capable of knowing, feeling, and acting. Deny that, and prayer becomes nonsense. Admit it, and prayer is of first importance. My limitations of mind and heart and will become less when I meet God face to face, and ponder in reverence the all-knowing, all-loving, all-powerful God. Our relationship is personal: child to Father, weak to strong, sinful to holy. Prayer is more than the approach of one person, with his own interests in mind, to God, in whom the interests of every person are present. No man lives alone, no man dies alone. We belong to a family. In prayer it is not for bread I plead, but for *our* bread. It is not my will, but God's will, and His will has to do with all of us. It is His kingdom, not my kingdom. At the very moment we beg forgiveness for our own trespasses, we are reminded that we may expect forgiveness even as we ourselves forgive. Jesus said, "Lead us not into temptation." Temptation itself is social. Our temptations involve others, whether the temptation be of the flesh, or of power, or of possessions. Much of our prayer is "together." We speak of corporate prayer. Much contemporary emphasis upon religion divorces the individual from the group, stresses the word "my," and seems to assume that if the individual gets right with God, salvation has come to him. But has it? The Biblical phrase is "Salvation to thy house." It involves family, community, nation, world. Prayer makes it clear that a cooperative task is before us, because the individual standing in the presence of God soon learns that God's concern for him is but part of God's concern for every human being, and that he, the worshiper, must be equally concerned with all, even as the God who is worshiped.

Prayer is transformation. Prayer is at times like the cold water into which heated metal is doused and tempered. There is a tempering quality about the prayer experience. Character is involved. Man possesses freedom of choice. This freedom is the gift of the Creator, a requisite of personality. It is freighted with danger. The choice can be good or evil. Prayer is often the ring in which a championship battle is fought. We would do God's will, we say, but we want a few qualifying sections in the contract. There are areas we propose to rule, areas in which our physical desires are to take precedence over our spiritual decisions. We sincerely seek God, but we want Him to understand that we are human, we live but once. In prayer, we, like David the King, are confronted by Nathan, who shouts, "Thou art the man." David could not behold Bathsheba naked, summon her to the palace, seduce her, and then send her husband to the battle front to die, and still sing the Psalm, "Create in me a clean heart, O God." Many a man goes down to defeat in the act of prayer. He cannot stand the scrutiny of God. The white light blinds him, but hot blood rules him. Prayer makes it clear, we can't have it both ways. Battles are won and lost on knees.

Praying for others has at times raised serious questions for me. Is it really true that our prayers have no influence upon God, that His will is determined? I reject this idea. He is a God who has ordained law. He works through law. Are we but insects drawn irresistibly to the flame, or pulped against the windshield of a madly driven automobile in early summer? Is it all planned, and are the plans irrevocable? Here, again, logic makes fools of us all. Is it more reasonable to assume that the All Knowing, whose purpose may be known to Him, is a dynamic Being making daily adjustments in order to realize that purpose? How can a man who has exercised his freedom and gone to a far country to spend his substance in riotous living expect to be received even as a hired servant when he returns to His Father's house, unless the Father from whom he has been estranged is there ready to rush down the road to greet him, and to cry, "My son who was lost is home again"? We can sit down and phrase our propositions. God knows everything; therefore, he does not need an intercessory prayer from me or you. Does it mean nothing to a loving God to know that His children love each other, and that there are some who love so much that they bring the needs of their dearest ones to the added attention of God Himself? I believe it does make a difference. Am I naïve when I remember my sons in prayer today just as I did when they were far away upon foreign battlefields?

My younger son was with the first outfits ashore on the Anzio beachhead. He was a chaplain. The landing ship was straddled by German bombs, and everyone thrown to the deck. He had noted that men attended church better after dangerous assignments. He was first on his feet and jokingly shouted, "I'll see all you birds at church on Sunday." A newspaper reporter was aboard and sent a story home. He mentioned my son's name and the censor passed it. I did not know where my boy was, but I learned one Sunday. I was rushing out of the South Station in Boston. I stopped to read a paper posted upon a bulletin board, and saw the story of the Anzio landing. I knew my son was in mortal danger. It proved to be the costliest bit of sand in all the world. I prayed for that boy and the others who were with him. I think God wanted me to. I did not pray that he alone be saved, nor for that matter that all the Germans be slain. I know what war involves. But I did talk to God about my son. Did it have any effect upon that battle? I know German fathers were praying for their boys. I say there are problems here. I do not know the answer, but I cannot rule out the possibility of Providence. I do believe God intervenes. I believe he intervened in history in the case of Jesus. Whether that was a part of a plan fully drawn at the dawn of creation, or was an act the sinfulness of men demanded or the love of God prompted, I do not know. I do know that Jesus came, and for me God has been uniquely and completely revealed to man. I believe that God as the sustainer of the universe is forever at work, that decisions are made daily, even as we in our little responsibilities make them. Whether my prayer for peace is heard, and another's prayer for victory in battle is influential, it is hard to prove. I believe the Father hears and knows and cares. Prayer enables me to trust, because it is in prayer that I seem best to apprehend the character of God. Whatever may be the result of my prayer in the matter of influencing God, certain it is that a receptive individual fully consecrated, who has given sufficient time for contemplation, is himself changed, made ready for God's will, and becomes a new person in dealings with his fellows.

We tend to become like what we pray for. We cannot pray for justice without thinking of justice and our own obligations. Similarly, in the question of righteousness, love, purity, peace. Paul enumerated the fruits of the spirit, and concluded, "Think on these things." Prayer is encounter, it is enrichment, it is thinking in the presence of God. When a man in prayer thinks of Jesus' command to love our enemies, or to walk a second mile, or to be merciful or pure in heart; when he knows that God considers the desires of the heart, prayer demands oblation. He must pay for the privilege of communion with God by being a just brother in his communion with his fellows. "Pray without ceasing" seems at first an absurd suggestion. It is not so strange when we think of our relationship with God as continuous and communion with Him as prayer.

I do not know how all our prayers could be answered. I pray for one thing, and a friend prays for its opposite. I know only that God is good, and that the closer I can be with Him, the greater the chance that I shall live more in accord with His will. Jesus came to do the will of His Father. That will is best learned in prayer. So I pray.

CHAPTER V

I Believe in the Church

I BELIEVE IN THE CHURCH. I love the Church, although intimately aware of its weaknesses, betrayals, and at times apostasy. No man who has been charged with heavy executive responsibility in the Church can be unaware of the fact that an institution composed of human beings, served by men and women limited as all humanity is, directed by persons subject to the temptations of power and of greed, is bound to reveal mankind not only at its best but at its worst. Power corrupts, and it will corrupt a bishop as well as a businessman, a church as well as a state. The greed that seeks property, the lust that is never satisfied until seduction, the madness that demands power — all have been present in an institution at once sacred and secular, but striving for ends that are divine.

For centuries, pope and bishop and priest were a hierarchy that conspired to rule, sought and secured vast wealth, and seemingly forgot that "he who would be greatest among you must become a servant."

The American representative to the Vatican, Mr. Louis R. Cass, Jr., wrote his chief, Mr. John M. Clayton, on April 21, 1849, "Communications have been made to me, from sources of the highest respectability, of the authority exercised by this ecclesiastical oligarchy, almost too monstrous for belief. . . . Being in complete possession of the courts of justice (if they deserve the name) and of the confessional, this body were enabled to convert all and every influence to their own personal and class aggrandizement, as they are accused of having done. In illustration of this system, I will quote from the law of fiducia, which is a matter of record, and familiar to every Roman. By this law, a dying man can give his property in trust to the priest attending his last moments, the secret words which the priest declares were uttered to him being considered his valid testament. Of course, such a law alone gives the priesthood the power of disinheriting any family and succeeding to any heritage."

The same spirit has been revealed in the activities of some men, Protestant and Roman Catholic alike. Unworthy ambition has led to political chicanery. In the struggle for ecclesiastical preferment, some men have stooped to the methods of a ward boss, while publicly summoning the people to the practices of the transformed heart. I know the Church well and doubt that there is any criticism to be offered that would bring new information to me.

But with it all, I believe in the Church. I sing:

> I love Thy Church, O God!
> Her walls before Thee stand,
> Dear as the apple of Thine eye,
> And graven on Thy hand.

I know that kings and empires have come and gone, but the Church lives on "a thousand years the same." I doubt that any reporter for the Roman paper *Acta Urbana* would have seen a story in the announcement, "The disciples were called Christians first at Antioch." His attention would have been directed to the household of the Imperial Legate or to the scandals associated with the pleasure gardens of Daphne. Of what possible interest to Roman readers was the little handful of Jews and Greeks who talked about one Christos and thus were nicknamed "Christians"? They met in a side street, sang hymns, shared in a strange supper, and listened to a man named Barnabas who had been sent up from Jerusalem to inquire of the work of this community that had grown up following the dispersal of the leaders after Stephen's death.

Antioch was one of the great cities of its day, a beautiful city, but a city content to seek satisfaction and pleasure, with little thought of the morrow, and less consideration of eternity. How could the Roman reporter know that these "Christians" were the first missionary church of a world religion, the first of "an endless line of splendor," a minority with a mission, charged with winning the world in the name of a World Saviour?

Is there a truer apprehension of the essential story of the Church than that found in the phrase of Vachel Lindsay, "an endless line of splendor"?

> An endless line of splendor,
> These troops with heaven for home,
>
> .   .   .   .
>
> This is our faith tremendous —
> Our wild hope, who shall scorn —
> That in the name of Jesus,
> The world shall be reborn!

"An endless line of splendor!"

A peasant girl, with a song on her lips. "My soul doth magnify the Lord, and my spirit hath rejoiced in God, my Saviour. . . . He hath . . . exalted them of low degree: He hath filled the hungry . . ."

A prostitute! "And there were with Him at the foot of the cross, Mary, His mother, *and* Mary Magdalene." It was she who came early on the first day of the week to the sepulchre. It is written, "But Mary stood without at the sepulchre weeping. . . . Jesus saith unto her, Mary. She turned herself and said unto Him, Rabboni: which is to say, Master." This is the beginning of the "line of splendor" — the clear, unequivocal response when He utters our name — Master!

A minority with a mission and a Master.

A fisherman with a sword, a coward shouting denial. And later, the risen Lord spoke to him: "Lovest thou me?" Shortly thereafter, here is the record: "But Peter, standing up with the eleven, lifted up his voice, and said unto them, Ye men of Judea, and all ye that dwell in Jerusalem, be this known unto you, and hearken unto my words."

A minority with a mission and a Master and a message.

Peter was to stand until they nailed him like his Lord to a cross. "Endless line of splendor"!

A tentmaker, Roman citizen, scholar, builder. "Who art Thou, Lord? I am Jesus whom thou persecutest." He had heard Stephen declare, "I see the heavens open and the Son of Man standing on the right hand of God." He had heard Stephen's prayer, "Lord, lay not this sin to their charge."

A minority with a mission, and a Master, and a message, and the certainty of life everlasting.

When they sought to put the faith into the compass of a creed, they said, "I believe in God" . . . yes, and "in Jesus Christ, His only Son our Lord" . . . yes, and in "the life everlasting." "The line of splendor" moved up. Were it the arena and the beasts of Rome, or the lash or faggots, hunger or thirst, or even the cross, the line moved on. The Christians knew they would never die.

Mary, the mother of Jesus, Mary Magdalene, Peter, Paul, Augustine, Francis, Bernard, Luther, Wesley, Livingstone, the men of the saddlebags, the classroom, the laboratory, the sick room and the surgery, the legislative hall, the market, the mine and the mill, the men and the

women who were determined "that in the name of Jesus,
the world shall be reborn."

I know that "the line of splendor" lost its luster at
times as the minority approached majority. Roman em-
perors bowed before the Cross. Property, power, and
prestige came to the Church. The Church took too much
thought for the morrow. Losing its life for His sake became a counsel of perfection, and practical men sought
incorporation papers for a new partnership: God, Mammon and Company. Church leaders became cautious.
They identified the *status quo* with the gospel. Kings
ruled by divine right, so they said, and the division of
society into nobles and serfs was ordained of God. Thus
feudalism became sacrosanct and advocacy of change
blasphemy.

But always within the fellowship there were those who
caught anew the spirit of the Lord. The Nazareth sermon
was repreached. The Savonarolas, the Joans, and the
Husses were burned; the Franciscans and the Wesleyans
were born. The scorn of tyranny leaped again from the
preaching of the prophets, from the Magnificat of Mary,
and the Acts of the Apostles.

Anne Morrow Lindbergh in a sensitive and significant
story tells of her visit to the reconstructed twelfth-cen-
tury Cistercian Abbey of Boquen in Brittany. She stood
looking up at a stone madonna, "sheltered in her niche
above the low arched door of the monastery." Beside her
was Dom Alexis, the monk, the founder and head of the
abbey, himself one of the "endless line of splendor." The

madonna had been carved by one of the brothers, he told her. "We call it Our Lady of Risk." Mrs. Lindbergh was startled by the unconventional title. "You mean," she said, "one must risk one's life — one must lose one's life to gain it?" "Yes," Dom Alexis answered, "Our Lady of Risk."

Perhaps personal experience and deep emotion become too strong for objective judgment when I face up to the question of the Church. It was in 1896 that a devoted Sunday School teacher in Los Angeles sent a postcard to a boy of five years of age who had been absent from the Children's Circle the Sunday before, telling him he was missed. Forty years later, the same lady, Miss Mary Davis, sent that boy a letter immediately following his election as a bishop. I was that boy and the postcard and the letter are kept among my treasures. I think of the thousands of devoted Church School teachers, among them my own mother reading the commentaries and the classics to make herself ready for the class of girls she would teach on Sunday. I think of a Wesleyan Chapel in Carn Brea Pool, Cornwall, England, and an altar where my father knelt as a young man of eighteen. His father was a mining contractor, a man of deep religious conviction, who lived among people who had heard John Wesley preach. My father at that age was not much interested in religion. One day, with his younger brother and his father, he was working hundreds of feet below the surface in the famous Dolcoath tin mine in Cornwall. Disaster came upon them. There was the terrible roar of falling rock. My father caught up his brother and carried him to a place of safety. It was bright as day. The rocks striking rocks lit up the underground workings. My father knew that his father, an experienced man underground, would find shelter beneath some ledge. Finally, there was silence and darkness. My father called out, "Strike a light, Father." There was no answer. My father understood. Two days later, they dug those boys out. My father had become a man. He had thought deeply. The following Sunday night he went to church, heard a simple sermon, and when the preacher asked for those who would accept Christ as Saviour to come and kneel at an altar, he did. For him God's love had become personal. He could sing the hymn John Wesley had written "For the Anniversary Day of One's Conversion":

> Then with my heart I first believed,
> Believed with faith divine;
> Power with the Holy Ghost received
> To call the Saviour mine.
> I felt my Lord's atoning blood
> Close to my soul applied;
> Me, me, He loved — the Son of God —
> For me, for me, He died.

He knew that night that his sins were forgiven, that God loved him, and that from that moment he would never be alone again. Christ had become a reality in his life. "Lo, I am with you alway" was more than a verse of Scripture. It was an experience. Intuitively, he knew that God does not coerce the soul; and in that experience he knew that his consent had brought new life, new assurance, and new power.

My father came to this dear land. At first he worked with his hands, and later many thousands worked for him. I am proud to record that he never left a mining camp without a church in it. At first he built them with his own hands, and later he contributed means to have them built. As my mother came to the close of her life, she wanted to revisit some of the mining camps in which she had lived as a bride, and so we visited them together. The last time I was with her was in such a camp at Marysville, Montana. The streets, once crowded with strong men and brave women, were deserted. The cabins, once happy homes, were long since abandoned. In imagination, my mother peopled the streets. Finally we walked together to a little church and entered it. I stood before a rude altar rail. My father had helped to place it there.

When I consider the Church, I am convinced of one fundamental fact. Differ as we may in our concepts of polity, in our theological emphases, in our dress, and in our practice, we are one, one in God's love. In that love, the goal of the Church becomes clear. It is to teach men to love God with heart, mind, and soul and to love neighbors as themselves. The basic purpose of the Church must be to deepen and to increase that love. Is not this the true meaning of Paul's statement: "God was in Christ reconciling the world unto Himself"?

I cannot define the Church. I am convinced, however, that the First and the Second Commandments, as defined so simply by Jesus, constitute the essential purpose of the Church. In so far as the proclamation of the faith results not alone in belief in God but in the actual love of God and love of neighbor, the Church realizes its goal. We think of the Church as an institution. It is. The Church may be more than an institution and it may be that many millions who have learned to love God and to love their brothers, who in a word are at one in thought with all those who do love God and brother, are also in the Church. I realize that stricter definition may be necessary. How can we train men for the ministry unless we have spelled out the meaning of the term "Church"? Nevertheless, I grow fearful when the search for strict definition begins.

Sincere, scholarly, saintly men who without question belong to the Church differ relative to the nature of the Church and are poles apart when discussing faith, sacraments, polity. How are we to interpret divisions at the Table of the Lord? I saw the Archbishop of Canterbury kneel during a communion service at the First Assembly of the World Council of Churches at Amsterdam, but he refrained from receiving Communion. Why must he deny himself the Sacrament in a service according to the rite of the Dutch Reformed Church? The Archbishop is a man of fine mind, Christian spirit, brotherly love, and extraordinary administrative ability. He occupies a position of great dignity and historical significance. Who can forget his conduct in the reading of the ritual in the coronation of Queen Elizabeth? This is no man of narrow mind and intolerant spirit. He is a Christian. But he "could not" and did not receive Communion. Why? At

Evanston, during the Second Assembly of the World
Council of Churches, many churches shared in the service
of communion at the First Methodist Church, among
them Lutherans and Anglicans. But my dear and highly
talented friends, Franklin Clark Fry, president of the
United Lutheran Church in the United States and the
present chairman of the Central Committee of the World
Council of Churches, and Henry Knox Sherrill, the pre-
siding bishop of the Protestant Episcopal Church in the
United States and one of the presidents of the World
Council, were not there. I had witnessed Dr. Fry refrain
from receiving Communion from the Archbishop of Canterbury when we shared in the service in the chapel at
Lambeth Palace in London. I inquired about it, and Dr.
Fry said, "I have never received Communion from hands
other than Lutheran." These are men of great ability, devout and dedicated servants of the Church, dear friends,
whose talents I covet and whose spirit and service are
an inspiration. What does it mean? I do not write
critically, but inquiringly. Are the bread and wine, these
precious symbols of the body and blood of our Lord, reserved for those who belong to a privileged or selected
few? When I read the words of invitation, "Ye that do
truly and earnestly repent of your sins, and are in love
and charity with your neighbors, and intend to lead a
new life, following the commandments of God, and
walking from henceforth in His holy ways, draw near
with faith, and take this holy Sacrament to your comfort;
and devoutly kneeling make your humble confession to
Almighty God," to me the words mean what they say, and

I receive all who come and share the sacred elements with them.

The Apostle Paul speaks of "one body and one Spirit," of "one Lord, one faith, one baptism, one God and Father of us all." If the supreme purpose of the Church is to bring all men to a place where they love God and their brothers, do we not find the Church wherever the grace of God as seen in Jesus Christ is present?

There is division when we face the question of ordination. I am frank to say that these divisions and the discussions associated with them are at once disappointment and irritation, especially when I hear the proud claims of some Protestant communions and realize that they are rejected by the Roman Catholic Church and in part by the churches of the Orthodox tradition. Is it but the fact that certain hands have not been placed upon the head of some dedicated young man at ordination that makes the difference? Is this the link essential to fellowship? If it is, then the problem is of easy solution. I would gladly kneel at any service where all that is believed to be present in an Anglican ordination might be communicated to all and all that is alleged to be present in any other ordination might be similarly bestowed. It would be for me a sacred and heart-warming moment to have the hands of Harry Emerson Fosdick placed upon my head and the independence of the Baptist tradition symbolically passed to me; and similarly to have received from Henry Sloane Coffin the rich traditions, the clear thought, and the democratic spirit of the Presbyterians; from Henry Knox Sherrill all that lies in the concept of the historic episcopate; and from Rufus Jones, if he were still with us, the insights of the silences, the concerns that come from intimate communion with the Eternal. Such a service would seem to meet the proposals of Canon Wedel in *The Coming Great Church*. He suggests, "The problem of an ecumenical ministry is not one of creation, but of recognition," and declares that "in some unmistakable way, recognition must be given to non-Episcopal ministries as true ministries of God." The Bishop of Chichester, the Reverend Dr. G. K. A. Bell, appears to agree. Referring to ministers of other communions, he writes, "What they lack is not ordination, but the special link with the apostolic ministry."

However, when I heard a distinguished scholar of the Russian Orthodox Church insist that it was not enough to share in such a service, but that I must accept the Orthodox theory of the ordination, then, of course, I could not honestly kneel. I do not believe there is an unbroken line of the properly ordained. Even if this were demonstrated, I cannot believe that the mere tactual fact of the physical placing of hands upon the head makes ordination valid.

The Central Committee of the World Council of Churches at its Toronto meeting in 1950 considered the difficult question of the nature of the Church. The debate for me became very trying. Not a few made reference to an old phrase, "true, healthy, and complete," when referring to the Church. In each case it seemed to me that the one who was stressing his theory of the Church was assuming that his own church was the true

Church, the healthy Church, the complete Church. It was not so stated, but it was surely to be implied that the way to reunion was for those of us who were not in the true, the healthy, and the complete Church to return. Finally, I arose and proposed an amendment to what is called "The Basis." The basis upon which we cooperate in the World Council of Churches is the statement, "The World Council is a fellowship of Churches that accept Jesus Christ as God and Saviour." I am not at all sure that this is the best phrasing of the basis of unity, because our Christian doctrine, if I understand it correctly, speaks of Jesus as the God-man. He was not only God, but also man. In Him the two natures were present. I do not wish to debate that. The Basis may someday be amended, but at present it constitutes the basis in fact upon which we cooperate. There were some present who thought me serious rather than satirical. I moved that we amend The Basis to read that the World Council is a fellowship of some true, healthy, and complete Churches in cooperation with some untrue, unhealthy, and incomplete Churches; and then suggested that if we would adopt that much of the amendment, it would be necessary to go further and strike out the word "fellowship," because the council under such circumstances would have ceased to be one; and finally I suggested that if that were true, it would be wise to strike out all reference to our blessed Lord, because we would have long since departed from His Spirit. I am sure that some thought that my suggestion was not only a revelation of ignorance and inability to apprehend the seriousness of the issue before us, but an expression of very bad manners. Nonetheless, the issue was brought out. It is present and we must face it. Of course, the logicians rush in. They insist there is a difference between the practices of a small emotional sect and the great Church of the centuries. Yes, I am sure there is. I know we must have definitions. I doubt, however, that the reunion of the churches will be based upon agreements that are reached in advance by those who wish to discuss theology and polity. I know we must know what we are doing when we ordain a man and I am sure this involves regulations. This is true in the case of swearing in the President of the United States or of appointing or of electing a judge. It is true in legislatures. Unfortunately, the debate takes us away from the fundamental purpose of the Church, which has to do with the love of God and the love of brother.

Once upon a time when the future of England was at stake, clergy were debating the question of what constitutes a proper haircut for a priest. The issue of tonsure may have been important then but hardly now. Debates of yesterday are matched today by such imbibing of abstractions that otherwise sane men appear to be intellectually intoxicated. The inevitable result is hang-over and headache. Erudite meets erudite, division continues, and sincere men reach diametrically opposite conclusions. What does the poor layman do?

I cannot think of the Church as a supernatural agency. To me it is a fellowship of men and women who have heard God in person say, "Follow me." Jesus knew that organization was necessary. Did he not choose the Twelve? He did establish a Church, and our unity is in fact greater than our diversity, no matter how vigorous the declaration of the diverse. He came that we might know the Father, and love Him. The Church strives to bring us to the seeking Father and, more, to send us in love to our brother. It is a fellowship that would have men love God and love each other. It is as simple as that. At least it is for me.

Thus, I find it difficult to become excited when I hear men talk of the machinery of organization as the vital matter. Episcopacy? Apostolic succession? No church without a bishop? Personally, I believe in the episcopal form of government. Historically, I think we had bishops from the very beginning. The episcopal system developed. Whether Christ intended that to be the only system of government within the Church He established is a theory not yet demonstrated. To insist that fellow ministers are not properly ordained or lack that particular link with the past is something I cannot accept.

I believe the Church must be the teacher of the principles of conduct. I believe it is the custodian of the message of the Master. I believe at times it must be a voice of judgment. I am sure it must be the herald of a new day. But, above all, the Christian Church must be the agency dedicated so to present Christ that men are indeed reconciled to God. "God was in Christ reconciling the world unto Himself."

Men come to God in different ways. Because I hold that we must bring our best when we come into the presence of God, I prefer formal services of worship. I desire beauty of music, the dignified reading of the Scripture, sincerity and simplicity in prayer, courageous and prophetic preaching. Cathedral and chapel have their places. I have seen soldiers receive Communion while kneeling in the mud. I have received Communion at Canterbury. If we could but be together more, common sense would do its healing work. This is happening in the ecumenical movement. Our association there makes visible the unity for which our hearts crave. We learn from each other and the corrective impact of collective thinking does its work. We witness and worship together. In ecumenical circles we are learning to study, to speak, to stand, and to serve together. It is along this road that we move to eventual unity. Still there are issues that divide us and they must be faced frankly.

In the message that was adopted in the Second Assembly of the World Council of Churches, this sentence occurs: "He will come again as Judge and King to bring all things to their consummation." True, the message had a strong social and evangelistic note, but at its close, reiterated its early statement: "We do not know what is coming to us. But we know Who is coming. It is He who meets us every day and who will meet us at the end as Jesus Christ our Lord." The assembly had given itself to the discussion of a noble theme, "Jesus Christ, the Hope of the World," and there were many references to the second coming of Christ.

Newspaper reporters who hold that normal life is seldom news seek out the controversial, the dramatic, the unusual; and understandably so. The officers and the delegates to the assembly were subjected to questioning, some significant, some stupid. Too few of the questioners had prepared themselves to ask penetrating questions. One reporter caught me by the arm as I was leaving one of the sessions and said, "Bishop, what about this second coming business?" I answered in haste, and a hasty answer is likely to provoke rather than to turn away wrath. I said, "To me it is a contradiction in terms. If Jesus is present now, and I believe He is, why discuss a second coming?" I heard from that from many quarters. One distinguished leader said, "Bishop, are you unacquainted with the Biblical teaching in this field; have you never looked into the eschatological question?" I thought of the long hours with the great theologian Albert C. Knudson of the Boston University School of Theology, and of the year we had given to a close study of Albert Schweitzer's *The Quest for the Historical Jesus,* which was eschatology with a vengeance. But why argue?

Eschatology is a theologian's word, and a very significant word at that. We must consider the "last things." What is ahead for the world? Is life upon this planet to end? Are we awaiting some frightful astronomical tragedy? The end of history? Such considerations did not weigh too heavily upon men of the last generation who were convinced of the inevitability of progress. But with the coming of the atomic and the hydrogen bomb and the real possibility of man committing suicide, we have been facing up to this question realistically. The early Christian did think of the impending end of things. He believed the Day of Judgment was imminent. Jesus did speak of coming again, and at first many believed Jesus would return during their lifetime. From time to time through history large numbers have awaited the end of the world — witness the terrifying days as the year A.D. 1000 approached.

It is a fearful subject to consider. If history is to end, is it to be a catastrophe? Is this part of the divine plan? What does all this mean? Is there to be a final judgment, and is judgment day to become more than a term to frighten the faithful who have become unfaithful?

Christians have believed in a transcendent order that is to replace the temporal order. We recall references to the final trumpet. In Matthew, the Twenty-fifth Chapter, is to be found the picture of humanity summoned before the Judge, judgment pronounced, with eternal joy and beatitude for some and eternal damnation for others. This is a serious matter, well worth careful thought. We think in terms of a heavenly fatherland. Our social obligations here are related to the compulsions of that eternal community. The City of God on earth is to be built in accord with the plans of the city that is celestial. Consequently, for the Christian, it is not a matter of working out the ideal society on earth experimentally, but of building in conformity with celestial blueprints. The Church becomes an expression of the heavenly community in time and upon the earth. Thus it becomes a social force of great power. There is the constant call to incarnate upon earth a society that is beyond earth, the society that is everlasting. Here is the summons to give life to love, to move from its easy pronouncement as morals to its active practice as message.

This is in no sense an adequate presentation of eschatology, and I am not seeking to do so. But I would like to consider some of the implications of contemporary theology, namely, that the Kingdom of God cannot be realized upon this earth or in history. This, to me, is a shocking and shattering insistence. When I pray, "Thy kingdom come, Thy will be done, on earth as it is in heaven," I am not awaiting the end of history for the consummation of the prayer. When I repeat these words, I mean what I say. The Kingdom for me is a social order in which the will of God is done in all the activities of men. I have dreamed of the day when God's will may so rule. I do not know how long the earth may last. Nobody does. A catastrophic collision of heavenly bodies may occur. I do not know. I cannot believe, however, that the Creator would have established a universe of law, only to bring it to its end in the chaos of explosive encounter. For me, there are ages upon ages ahead. When gunpowder came, not to mention the long bow and the battering ram, poison gas, and other hellish instruments of war, the end was predicted. Man would wipe out the race, it was argued. Of course, there is a difference now, since a sufficient number of hydrogen bombs might do just that. Disease might devastate the earth, and civilization may be consumed in the fires of hydrogen blast. Personally I do not believe it.

Yes, I know man sins. I have but recently completed

the first volume of Sir Winston Churchill's *History of the English-Speaking Peoples.* Is there a tale written with skill more consummate, phrasing more expressive, and understanding deeper? It is a story of sinful men, a record of murder and rapine, of treachery and debauchery, but out of it all emerged Parliament and political freedom, and a truer justice than man has known. Had a man been writing when Edward II was murdered in bestial torture, he might well have said, "The Kingdom! Nonsense. The sons of Adam, cursed by original sin, are doomed and the Kingdom cannot be realized in history." I shall be told I do not know what the scholar means by the end of time. Perhaps, perhaps not. I am simply stating that this teaching is a teaching that short-circuits the flow of social justice. It is a factor in directing the masses to the materialist, who, without a Lord's Prayer, turns to a man who saw religion as but an opiate and summons the people to build the classless society and abolish the exploitation of man by man.

I am still ready to speak of the Kingdom in its social aspects, as defined following the First World War when we prayed with passion, "Thy kingdom come," and thought of it as coming here and now. "It would be a cooperative social order in which the sacredness of every life was recognized and everyone found opportunity for the fullest self-expression of which he was capable; in which each individual gave himself gladly and whole-heartedly for ends that are socially valuable; in which the impulses to service and to creative action would be stronger than the acquisitive impulses, and all work would be seen in terms of its spiritual significance as making possible fullness of life for all men; in which differences of talents and capacity meant proportional responsibility and ministry to the common good; in which all lesser differences of race, of nation, and of class served to minister to the richness of an all-inclusive brotherhood; in which there hovered over all a sense of the reality of the Christlike God, so that worship inspired service, as service expressed brotherhood." * These were the days of the so-called social gospel. It is said that contemporary eschatology gives just as great social drive. I doubt it. I think much of contemporary social drive is a carry-over from the day when it was believed that dedicated men, using their God-given reason, could be empowered by God Himself to take the revealed will of God as seen in Jesus with sufficient seriousness to give effect to His will, in a word, to build a Kingdom of God on earth.

But I must be fair. Karl Barth, whose brilliant mind has made such amazing contributions to contemporary thought, and whose courage led him to stand up against Hitler, set down certain theses. Who can deny the social power that lies in them? Barth wrote,† "The Church is a people consisting of those who have found in Jesus Christ their own comfort and hope and the comfort and hope

* The Committee on the War and the Religious Outlook, *The Church and Industrial Reconstruction* (New York: Association Press, 1920), pp. 31-32.

† Karl Barth, *The Church and the Political Problem of Our Day* (New York: Charles Scribner's Sons, 1939).

of the whole world, and who therefore have discovered their service in bearing witness before the world, which without Him is lost, to Jesus Christ in His offices of Prophet, Priest and King. . . . True witnessing to Jesus Christ occurs necessarily in the unity of two things, a definite repetition of the confession of Him as the One who has come to us as Son of God and Saviour and will come again, and of the actualizing of this confession in definite decisions in relation to those contemporary questions which agitate the Church and the world. . . . The political problem of 'our day' is the problem of German National Socialism, which directs itself to the whole contemporary world, and to the contemporary Church. . . . The double character of National Socialism as a political experiment and as a religious institution of salvation shuts out any possibility of dealing with the question it puts 'only' as a political question and not, indirectly and directly, as a question of faith as well. Consequently in no event can the Church adopt a neutral attitude to the political problem of today." Professor Barth developed these theses and finally wrote, "If it is true that no peace is possible between witnessing to Jesus Christ and the sovereignty of National Socialism, then it follows that the Church may and should pray for the suppression and casting out of National Socialism, just in the same sense as in former times and when confronted by a similar danger she prayed for the 'destruction of the bulwarks of the false prophet Mohammed.' " This is sufficient evidence, at least in the case of one mind, that the Church can confront the political problems of its day courageously and creatively. Perhaps Barth is better than his theology.

When the Church sees its goal as the increase of the love of God and the love of brother, it is pledged to the expression of that love in the enthronement of God's will in the social order. The ethical ideals of the prophets and the moral demands of Jesus must be more than pronouncement. They must become practice.

The Social Creed of the Churches is discounted in some quarters today, but it was the very proclamation of that creed that was decisive in the transformation of American business practice. The morality of contemporary economic enterprise differs today from that of 1900 as day differs from night.

Of discussion there is no end, whether the subject be that of the nature of the Church, the eucharist, or the ministry. J. Robert Nelson, the new dean of the Vanderbilt School of Theology, has considered these questions in a brilliantly written book entitled *The Realm of Redemption*. Its subtitle is "Studies in the Doctrine of the Nature of the Church in Contemporary Protestant Theology." He treats of such themes as "The Origin of the Church," "The Church and the Holy Spirit," "The Church's Relation to Christ," "The Word of God as the Church's Authority," "The Sacraments and the Ministry," "Salvation in the Church," "The Church's Essential Unity," and "The Church and Eschatology." He tells us that there is a "profound longing for unity," but even at the organizational meeting of the World Council of Churches in 1948 "lurking behind the scenes, so to speak.

frustrating every facile scheme for attaining unity was the ancient theological question, now made more urgent than ever: what is the Church?" He concludes, "So long as this problem remains unsolved, and until all Christians understand what is fully intended when the word, 'Church,' is spoken, the efforts to realize the unity of the One Body of Christ will lead to only an approximation of the ideal." He canvasses the views held by the scholars and concludes, "It is utterly unrealistic even to think that such a synthesis might be possible," and tells us, "This work is intended to be a synopsis, not a synthesis, of the foremost ideas and beliefs concerning the Church which are now current." If after twenty centuries of Christian history the views are still as diverse as his study shows them to be, then it may be that Dr. Nelson moves into more constructive proposals when he says, "A word of caution, based on my own experience in writing this book, might well be offered to the reader at this point. It is very easy to become so absorbed in theological problems relating to the Church that one unconsciously ignores the plain fact that the Church is made up of people rather than of doctrines and traditions. These are the ordinary Christian folk in every land, who have little or no concern for problems of theology, but whose worship and work are indispensable to the existence of the Church in any locality. It is for their ultimate benefit, and not for the intellectual delight of the theologically-minded, that the questions posed in the course of this study need eventually to be answered."

I believe in the Church. I think of the faithful men and

women who have experienced the love of God. They
have knelt at church altars. They have studied in church
classes. They have worshiped in church services. They
have read the Scriptures and prayed. They have sung the
hymns of the faith. They have learned to love one another and to serve even the least of these. The nature of
the Church is likely to be apprehended better by partici-
pating in its life than by long debate concerning its history.

The Church in which I believe is not an abstract en-
tity conjured up by the so-called scholar. The bookshelves
sag as speculative volume follows speculative volume
and finds its place among its fellows. Millions of words
have been written to explain what Jesus meant when He
said, "Upon this rock I will build my church." When do
we reach a definition that will satisfy? I think the answer
is "Never." I must start with a little congregation, a fellowship composed of human beings who have learned to
love God and each other because they have come to
know His blessed Son, who is for us the Way, the Truth,
and the Life. A little more time contemplating the
meaning of the Sermon on the Mount or the Thirteenth
Chapter of First Corinthians is likely to result in a larger
harvest of the fruits of the spirit. I sometimes think that
too many persons who formulate theology move from the
undergraduate classroom to the graduate classroom and
on to the professor's platform and study, far from the
realities of social struggle and the problems of the parish.
They are masters of technical jargon who read and re-
read the theoretical dissertations of their fellows. They

were described by Erasmus in *In Praise of Folly*. Of course there are notable exceptions. I think of Reinhold Niebuhr and the great debt Church, nation, and world owe to his brilliant thought. He is one of the most influential theologians and I know of no one more intimately acquainted with the social struggle of our day. I realize that our theological schools must become the intellectual center of the Church and that these discussions must go on and on. But?

Theological discussion is difficult for the average layman and average minister to understand, but understand we must. There is a faith and the faith must be phrased. I know this. Perhaps the difficulty lies in the fact that even among the intellectuals there is pride, sometimes an offensive pride. The academicians pride themselves in phrasing some new term compounded of Greek or Latin words. They establish a new school of thought which is to be dismantled by the next generation of speculators. Too many of these men live apart and the regenerating message of love is lost to the masses, who turn to the revolutionary manifestoes of force.

How much more we need to turn to the Christ Himself, and begin with His commanding simplicity. What did He do? At the first sermon in Nazareth, He said, "The Spirit of the Lord is upon me, because He hath anointed me to preach the Gospel to the poor; He hath sent me to heal the broken-hearted, to preach deliverance to the captives, and recovering of sight to the blind, to set at liberty them that are bruised, to preach the acceptable year of the Lord." Then He turned to the task of healing the sick. The early American talked much about the "pursuit of happiness." Jesus discussed the same theme in the Beatitudes: "Happy is the man who is poor in spirit." Have we sought the goal by the wrong road? If Jesus is God incarnate, would we not do better to consider His Way, in fact? His Truth? His Life?

I have often wondered what Jesus would think of a theological debate in which His nature was under discussion. What would He think of our consideration of the Church? What would be His reaction to creed, the Apostles' Creed, for instance, in which the word "love" is not mentioned. It was a new commandment that He gave unto us, that we should love one another as He loved us. What would He think of our church services, from the Mass with its grandeur, its music ascending in ecstasy, the doctrine of transubstantiation, the tinkling of bells, the genuflecting, the priesthood, to the ruder service in a barnlike auditorium where the most obscurantist teaching is bellowed, the music sometimes like current jazz, and emotions so frayed that audiences cease to be rational? What of the complacent liberal and the intolerant fundamentalist? What of all of us? He said, "Take up my cross. Follow me." Have we lost sight of Him?

I love the glorious cathedrals, the aesthetic satisfaction of pillar and clerestory, of stained glass and soft light, and of music well-nigh heavenly. I respond in joy to the procession, its color — the crucifer holding high the cross. I like the words before the sermon, "In the name of the Father, the Son, the Holy Spirit." But, where is He? What does He demand of us? "Go sell all that thou hast." Are alabaster boxes to be broken as His wearied feet are anointed? Or must we think Judaslike in terms of the treasury? Yes, I am enamored of organization; too much of my life has been given to it. I know He said, "Judge not that ye be not judged," and I would not violate that command. But there are others. "Love your enemies." How? Don't pray on the street corner to be seen of man. Cry out alone, kneeling before the Creator. Do we build upon the sand or upon the rock? It is all very confusing, not to say terrifying.

But next Sunday morning millions will enter our churches and our church schools. Faithful ministers and priests will take their accustomed places, sermons will be preached, Scripture read, prayers offered, men and women will go forth inspired. Inspired to do what? Enter debate concerning the nature of the Church? I hope not. If they are inspired to worship and love God, to love and serve their fellows and to do so in the name of Jesus Christ our Lord, I have reason to believe in the Church.

Was Robert Browning right? Is life just "our chance at the prize of learning love"? Perhaps.

It may be our only chance. John Wesley regarded it so. I think that position is justified by Biblical teaching unless one reasons from the fact of a God of love who in love sent His Son to preach a new commandment. Then I find it difficult to believe that there is one moment of judgment and the future is determined forever. I hold that God is just, but justice itself requires more than sentence at the close of a few years of living when that

sentence involves forever. I know there is great evangelistic power in the enunciation of the statement to accept God now or be damned forever. I know great and
sincere men have said, "Repent now before it is too late.
Accept Him now or take on hell forever." But for me it
cannot be. The doctrine of hell gave the priestly class
great power in the Middle Ages, and it was used to
amass property until at last the Church was the greatest
of landowners. The supreme pontiff was king as well as
priest, ruler not servant, playing the game hierarchies
have done and do. Who is the saved person? I have met
some of them, cold, calculating, respectable. But I remember Jesus saw the publican. He knew the scribes and
the Pharisees. He was crucified with the religious as well
as the Roman soldiers looking on. No, the Church must
proclaim a message in harmony with its purpose, that of
loving God and of loving brother.

Jesus is for me the hope of the world, this world, and
the next world. I believe in the Kingdom of God on
earth realizable in time. I see the Church as an agency,
a fellowship, dedicated to one glorious purpose, that of
bringing men to Christ. Let them stand in His presence
for a moment and then they will kneel, kneel to pledge
their all. He demands absolute obedience. This at least
is reason for the Church and, for me, a satisfying reason.
I am not afraid to let love work its transformation in the
community of intelligent men who have met love at an
altar in the Person of Jesus.

CHAPTER VI

I Believe in the Forgiveness of Sins

THE CHAPTER HEADINGS so far have been phrased like the affirmations of a creed, beginning with the words "I Believe." I believe in the forgiveness of sins. I also believe in the free mind, in the free society, seeking the truth that frees. Are these statements contradictory? Is it possible for the man who believes in the free mind to repeat a creed without mental reservation? It depends upon the definition of creed. If we regard creed as final statement, never to be questioned, and sacrosanct, the man pledged to the free mind faces a dilemma. I do not think creeds are to be so regarded.

Creedal statements have at times troubled me. I recognize the necessity of formulating the faith. What is it we believe? Obviously there must be an answer. It is less the formulation that troubles me than the use that is made of the formulation.

Many people want things settled. I can understand that. I have always loved order. I want all my books in their places, so that I can walk into the library in the dark and find a particular volume. I like a clear desk. A cluttered desk suggests a cluttered mind. I know, of course, that this cannot be true, because men like William Allen White and Hemingway and Berdyaev, to name widely different personalities, wrote orderly material at desks that appear from photographs to be covered with debris.

Nevertheless, it is proper to ask what you mean when you say, "Accept Christ." Who was Christ? If the answer is that He was the Son of God, it is proper to inquire in what way He differs from other sons of God. Why did He Himself object to being called "good"? How did He grow in wisdom and in stature and in favor with God and man, if the creedal affirmations are true? Yes, we need the creeds. They are valuable for teaching purposes, and their repetition in the service of worship is significant.

What are these creeds? Were they not man-made? Did they not emerge from bitter debate? How much did the money of Hosius have to do with the formulation of the Creed of Nicea? If a statement is but the meeting of minds and represents the best compromise possible at a given time, why do we hold the creedal statement in such reverence and ostracize the brother who cannot accept all of it or who demands revision? I am glad the Constitution of the United States can be amended, and I am equally glad that the process of amendment is deliberate and delayed. So, too, a creed. It must not be regarded as sacrosanct in the sense that it may not be questioned.

In this connection what do we do with Jesus Himself? He said, "It was said of old unto you . . . but I say unto you." True, He did not come to destroy the law, and the old was not destroyed; but the new carried on beyond the old and differed from it as day from night. "Thou shalt not commit adultery." Jesus knew the Ten Commandments. He also knew men. He therefore said, "He who looketh upon a woman unto lust hath already committed adultery with her in his heart." When He confronted the ancient practice of an eye for an eye and a tooth for a tooth, He said, "No, love your enemies." He commanded us to forgive, not seven times but seventy times seven. His was the type of mind that takes the principle and makes it regnant. He knew that it must be applied specifically, but was careful never to treat the specific in such fashion that it became the principle.

Creeds must be seen for what they are, namely, carefully phrased expressions of certain aspects of faith; approximations — because the finite mind can never fully comprehend the infinite. Creeds are not to be questioned lightly, not to be set aside casually. Personally, I prefer reverent disagreement to unthinking agreement.

I am not ruling out revealed truth. Assuming the fact of God as I do, it is reasonable, from my point of view, to hold that the Eternal Mind can make His thought known to mortal men. I believe He has done this. He has done it through the centuries. The revelation has been progressive. The men to whom He revealed Himself were human beings, limited as all men are limited. The revelation was conditioned by their ability to understand, and their reports bear evidence of the limitations that current events, current thought, and current practice evoke. Take the cosmology accepted by the Old Testament writers, for instance; or the belief in demons; or Paul's attitude toward women. To hold that Paul's advice on women is truth revealed by God and binding upon all is as sorry as to hold that God commanded the Jews to commit atrocities on their enemies in war. Nonetheless, truth is revealed. The Bible is the supreme revelation of the Eternal in writing and constitutes a sufficient source and ground for the formulation of faith. Creeds based upon that revelation are not only important but entitled to respect.

The supreme revelation of the Eternal is found in Jesus. John Baillie, scholar and teacher, one of the presidents of the World Council of Churches, concluded his brilliant and satisfying volume, *The Idea of Revelation in Recent Thought,* with these words:

> In the Old Testament it is often said that no man has seen God, and indeed God is made to say, "There shall no man see me and live." This is taken up in the New Testament, but with an addition. St. John says, "No man hath seen God at any time; the only begotten Son, who is in the bosom of the Father, he hath made him known." And, according to St. John, Jesus Himself said in answer to

Philip's request to show him the Father, "He that hath seen me hath seen the Father." That is the whole essence of the Christian faith, that Jesus Christ hath shown us the Father, that in Him there has been revealed to us all we need to know about our ultimate concern. "All we need to know." There is much that we do not know. Now we know in part, as St. Paul says, and it may sometimes seem to us to be only a very small part. Now we see only, he says again, as in a mirror dimly. The clouds and thick darkness remain, and the light piercing them sometimes seems scant enough. But it is the Light of the World. It is more light than we are ever likely to use. It is enough to see to do our work by, and until we have done our work we have no cause to repine. When our work is done, it is promised that we shall know even as we are known and that we shall see face to face.

Many Christians hold that it is only the truth revealed in Jesus that will make us free. I believe that Christian faith when understood and practiced does free the soul, but I believe also that truth from any source contributes to freedom. Truth is one. It is not Indian truth, Chinese truth, Russian truth, Jewish truth, or American truth. It is truth! Truth is like light. Truth emancipates, strikes the shackles from the imprisoned mind, and sets the prisoner free. The truth that comes from the rack of test tubes, the mathematicians' tables, the telescope, from research, no matter where, frees. The man whose brooding mind enables him at last to set down a formula, a few letters with plus or minus signs, an exponent or two, and thus state a law has contributed to truth. This truth frees. A man who has discovered truth may not accept the Christian faith in its entirety; he may deny immortality and reject much that I hold dear and sacred; but if what he has discovered is true, it frees. It must be accepted. The false must be rejected. It is by the road of truth that we march to the land of freedom.

All of this is to say that the open mind is requisite to peace of soul. It is not simply drawing larger circles to take in those who draw the smaller circles to shut us out. Edwin Markham, bless his great soul, was right enough. We must have that type of charity. But it is the open mind that is wanted. This does not mean that I do not hold fast to my faith. Not at all. But if Dead Sea scrolls are discovered, I must be ready for such revision in my understanding of the thought of Jesus as the new truth demands.

I remember a class in theism at the University of Southern California. Professor John G. Hill had taken us through a careful study of Darwin's thought and the revisions in religious thinking that the concept of evolution necessitated. I was a student like one of those who later embarrassed me with questions. I asked Professor Hill, "Is the evolutionary process ended?" His answer was, "Of course not." Then I queried, "Is it not conceivable that a time may come when there will be life upon this planet as much beyond man as man is at present beyond the ape?" Professor Hill replied, "Yes, that is quite conceivable." The door was now open for the real question. "If that be true, Professor, what happens to our present idea of Christ as the incarnate Son of God? Would the man that is to be think of Jesus as we think of the primitives?" Perhaps it was an irreverent question, but it was an honest one. Professor Hill might have reported me to the Methodist authorities and have raised questions concerning my fitness for the ministry. He did nothing of the kind. On the contrary, he examined the question. He reviewed the life of Jesus and asked, "Can you think of anyone or any being that is to come as a fuller revelation of God than Jesus was?" We saw Jesus not only as God incarnate but as One who revealed in His person the love Jesus demands: greater love hath no man than this, that a man lay down his life for his friend. We saw the Cross in all of its redemptive majesty. We heard again the line from the ancient hymn, "Died He for me who caused His pain?" The point here is that the professor revealed the free mind and respected the immature mind of a student. In such revelation, I think he was revealing the mind that was in Christ Jesus. It was an open mind.

It is hard to keep the mind open. Everywhere, in every organization, the demand for conformity to the thought and the practice of the past is present. In the Church, too, there are those who, like the Communist, insist that deviation is disloyalty; dissent is treason. It is conform or die. Mark Guy Pearce, the great English preacher, when visiting Los Angeles said, "Your ways are better, but we like ours best." There is something to be said for that, but when the ways we like best are no longer productive of social good, they must go. There are moments

when men must risk their lives, their fortunes, their
sacred honor, and write a Declaration of Independence,
beginning with the words, "When in the course of human events, it becomes necessary . . ." Declarations of
Independence are necessary not only in the political
realm but in the ecclesiastical and the economic, too. At
Concord, Massachusetts, a stone bears the poignant lines:

> They came three thousand miles, and died,
> To keep the Past upon its throne;
> Unheard, beyond the ocean tide,
> Their English mother made her moan.

Determined to keep the past upon the throne, con-
formists court-martialed General Mitchell, contemporary
railroad executives plan to meet competition of the air-
lines by raising passenger rates until first-class travel is
prohibitive. This is like the ecclesiastical mind that pre-
fers the easy working of the denominational machinery
to the harder adjustments necessary to demonstrate Christ
and unity in ecclesiastical polity.

The open mind is particularly necessary when we consider the forgiveness of sin.

During World War II, I visited Greece and was the
guest of the Regent, Archbishop Damaskinos. He was a
giant in stature and his courage matched his physique.
One afternoon we drove out from Athens into the country and he talked of the Germans and of the occupation.
He said, "They were the best-disciplined soldiers in the
world. They were under orders not to molest Greek
women. Their orders were obeyed, and we are thankful

for that. But they planned to destroy us. They starved us deliberately and ruthlessly. Children died in the streets and death visited nearly every home." His resentment was all the more terrible because of the very restraint of his utterance.

Finally I said, "Your Beatitude, tell me how you reconcile your Christianity and your patriotism. Our Lord commanded us to love our enemies. You are a patriot and King. How can you act as the head of the Church and as the head of the State?" He was silent for a time, and then he said, "It is well-nigh impossible. I cannot hate and love at the same time. As a Christian, I tried to keep hatred out of my heart and to seek reasons that would explain the crimes of our enemy. As a patriot, there were moments when I felt we should rise and, if possible, destroy every one of them. I know all of us have come short of the glory of God, and I honestly seek to understand and to forgive, and thus make myself ready for love. But I must tell you very frankly, at times my patriotism rules and my anger alarms me. It is then I must struggle hardest to remember that I am a man of God as well as a man of Greece."

It is not easy to forgive. God is not only a God of love, but of necessity a God of righteousness and of justice.

A discussion of forgiveness of sin, like a consideration of prayer, involves the question of theism. If there is no God, then there is no one, save our fellow men, to forgive. I assume the fact of God, a morally obligated Supreme Being, Creator and Sustainer of the universe, all-knowing, all-powerful, all-loving, just and righteous. My faith is based on two fundamental propositions: one, nothing can separate me from the love of God; and two, God was in Christ reconciling the world unto Himself.

I believe I am free to choose what I believe to be right or wrong. In fact, I am free to take my own life. Economic and social conditions, physical inheritance and disease are of great influence, and to a degree my actions are determined by factors other than my will, but in the large I know that I possess freedom and am rightfully held responsible for my conduct. There is, of course, a line that is crossed and responsibility ends — such as loss of mind, or when tortured, drugged, and brainwashed until normal faculties cease to function. I must reject theories of conduct based upon physiological or economic determinism. For me, determinism is out, moral responsibility is in.

Sin is always individual. Responsibility is personal. True enough, the consequences of sin are social. My sins, nevertheless, are mine. I, a free person, decide to do what I know to be wrong. It is true that some sin results from ignorance, and thus acquisition of knowledge is indicated, but most sin is born of pride and of greed. The will of God is clear enough for most of us. Selfishness is the chief contributing factor to disobedience. A man knows there is something higher and better and yet he deliberately disobeys. Milton sings "Of Man's Disobedience." Basically we deal here with disloyalty. Most of us know that goodness inheres in loyalty and unselfishness, but we prefer our own way, our own desires.

Jesus made it clear. He saw sin as hatred of brother. He found it in lustful desire. It was present in the substitution of display and pretense for simplicity and sincerity; in the attempt to serve two masters; in sitting in judgment upon a brother rather than surveying one's own lack; in the failure to trust God and to obey Him; in the worry that bears testimony to doubt; in the rejection of meekness, purity, and self-righteousness; in the refusal to forgive, or to walk the second mile. If a man does not love his brother, whom he has seen, how can he love God, whom he has not seen?

Why didn't God create the universe without sin? There is only one answer: He could have done so, and man would have been but a pawn upon a chessboard. Pawns are not responsible for moves of the great Player. We must be free to be persons, and being free, we are charged with making decisions. Some of them result from the self-assertive qualities with which we are endowed, from the instinct of self-preservation that is innate. Schweitzer sees "reverence for life" as the basic ethical principle. I agree. But antecedent to that is the will to live. This is native to humanity. All these characteristics enter into a consideration of sin. God's revelation of His own nature, and man's capacity to think in terms of others, to transcend his own interests, in a word, to die for an ideal or a loved one, must be taken into account.

W. F. Ashley-Montagu, in *On Being Human,* declares, "Every human being is a problem in search of a solution." The problem inheres in his freedom. He may choose to do good. He may choose to do evil.

Obviously, a righteous being cannot condone unrighteousness. Eugene O'Neill in *Desire Under the Elms* traces sin to its consequences. He does not sit in judgment. He writes with scientific precision. Sin results in consequences. We reap what we sow. After the tyrant comes the deluge.

The Church has taught different theories of forgiveness. There were those who bogged down in a dualism that assumed God and the Devil in battle for the souls of men. There was a Kingdom of Evil, as well as a Kingdom of God. Sin meant that man of his own volition had become a citizen of Satan's kingdom. He was held as a hostage until a ransom was paid. Satan was like a kidnaper who refused to free sinners until the payment was made. There was but one ransom of sufficient amount and that was God's own Son. Modern man rejects the dualism of yesterday, repudiates the idea of Satan, and therefore discards theories that assume heavenly warfare in which God and the Devil are engaged.

There were long periods, not yet ended in some quarters, when satisfaction for sin was a prerequisite to forgiveness. Penance was required. Sin was regarded as a debt. The debt must be paid or the sinner punished. But the debt was so great it became apparent that man could never pay it. So the theologians spun the theory that only an infinite Being could make satisfaction for sin that in itself had become infinite. In this theory Christ is offered as satisfaction. The debt is paid. Man is saved.

There were those who thought in legal terms, and held that penalty must be exacted. Penalty involves punishment. So Christ was offered as a substitute. We hear much of the substitutionary theory of the atonement. This theory is to me immoral. If Jesus paid it all, or if He is the substitute for me, or if He is the sacrifice for all the sin of the world, then why discuss forgiveness? The books are closed. Another has paid the debt, borne the penalty. I owe nothing. I am absolved.

I cannot see forgiveness as predicated upon the act of someone else. It is my sin. I must atone. First, by repentance. Not being sorry in general, but sorry in particular. I must repent of my sins, and stand before my Creator in contrition, knowing that I, when I come to myself as did the Prodigal, may return to my Father's house certain of welcome, assured of love. But the years in the far country, the separation from my Father, constitute a fact. Consequences follow.

I must confess my sins, certainly. Have I stolen, then restitution is required. Zaccheus determined to restore fourfold. It is not enough to kneel at an altar and to become the recipient of God's forgiving love. More is required. I must get right not only with God but with my brother. Tragically enough we can never fully repay. Have we blinded a man? How can his sight be restored? We cannot keep stolen goods, but what of the years that have been stolen from others when our actions have denied them opportunity? Forgiveness requires that we make amends for the trespass, and also forgive those who trespass against us. Making ready for forgiveness is something of a chore. There is no ledger account in the great assize that bears my name, with my sins down the debit side and a balancing credit entry indicating Christ's sacrifice is sufficient for my sin. It is rather an open account that involves my life and its continuing relationship to God and man. We must think of the role of Christ in the realm of forgiveness in terms of love.

The incarnation is a doctrine that affirms God was in Christ reconciling the world unto Himself. Not that God had to be changed, that His love had abated, that he was alienated. On the contrary, Christ reveals a God who is the same yesterday, today, and forever, a Being forever seeking His children. It is they who must be changed, not He. Hence, the idea of forgiveness or salvation is not one of penalty, sacrifice, ransom; it does not posit a jealous, vindictive, Shylockian deity. No, Jesus reveals a God who must be known, adored, worshiped, obeyed. This is the first step toward salvation and forgiveness. No wonder Jesus taught us to pray. God is to be loved, talked to, lived with. Man cannot with any sense of propriety violate the commands of a Being at once so holy and so loving.

Jesus manifested the essentials. He lived a life of absolute trust in God, and of unfailing obedience to His will. John said, "Grace and truth came through Jesus Christ." Jesus suffered as we suffer, and more. The crown of thorns was cruel, as were the cries of the mob calling for crucifixion. The nails were nails in fact, not symbols. The spear thrust was agony, and the thirst was torture. In the last moment he cried, "Into Thy hands I commend my spirit." The crucifixion where, in loyalty to His Father's will, Jesus died was more than a death upon a cross; it was the revelation in a Person of the love of God from which we cannot be separated. That love demands soul, life, all. We saw it in Jesus. It compels response. God and sinners are reconciled not by sacrifices, ransom, the payment of penalty, but by love. No wonder Jesus could say, "Be of good cheer, I have overcome the world." He had.

The legalistic approach to forgiveness has made pagans of us all. We have attributed to a God of holiness, love, and righteousness characteristics and conduct that contradict His essential nature. We speak of Him as "jealous," a Being of wrath, a Person who seems almost to delight in punishing His creatures. He visits the sins of the fathers upon the children and the children's children. He sends plague upon the first-born of the Egyptians. Jonah goes so far as to say God repented of the evil He intended to do.

Sin is less the violation of law than it is the rejection of love. God is love. We do not repent because we fear an awful and an avenging deity. We repent because our hearts are broken. We have violated love, not law. Jesus revealed a God whose love is unfailing, who eagerly awaits the sinner's cry for forgiveness.

Nevertheless, we must face up to the requirements of justice and of righteousness. God cannot be just and treat the man who is honest as He treats the thief. He cannot look upon the acts of Hitler or of Stalin, or upon our own acts that repudiate love of brother, without the justice of His Being calling for consequences. We speak of punishment, but what is punishment? If sin is alienation from God, and the deliberate violation of His will, is there greater punishment than to live so alienated and in such continuous violation? Does not conscience exact its toll? But is that all? Surely not. Would not death be merciful? It would appear that a tyrant who must live on, plagued by the nightmarish memories of his crimes, would be suffering far more for sin than simply to forfeit existence.

Take the case of Judas, who took his own life as well as betrayed his Lord! Is the action of betrayal to determine his place throughout all eternity? If a thief may repent in the last moment and be that day with Christ in paradise, is such repentance to be forever decisive? I simply cannot reconcile the conception of hell with a God of love. Is any act, the most heinous, justly punished when the verdict is eternal damnation? God is still God, still a Being of justice and of love. Even if payment in terms of punishment is required to meet the demands of justice, does not love involve eventual regeneration, the eventual victory of love itself?

Love never fails, we are told. Do we imprison a soul at death in a prison that love cannot penetrate? Does the command to visit those in prison end when a heart stops beating? Man can turn from God's love; he can reject its benefits and live apart, but God's love pursues him — a Hound of Heaven. No greater punishment can be conceived than that of living in rebellion against God, and to do so in the face of continuous offer of forgiveness!

The old pictures of men suffering the torments of hell may have kept some from sinning. Fear of hell gave the hierarchy control over much of mankind; but fear is not the motive upon which contemporary man relies to elicit goodness. The ridiculous depths to which so-called thinkers can descend are plumbed by discussions about little children who were unbaptized. These little ones were damned even as sinners in the hands of an angry God. What has happened to the mind of a normal man who can allow alleged logic to drag him to the conclusion that a lovely baby is to suffer eternal damnation because a parent failed to arrange for baptism or deliberately decided baptism was a matter for adult decision? Logic makes fools of the logicians.

The Christian movement began with the summons to repent. That is the first step toward forgiveness. We speak of a man being saved, and as Protestants, we declare, "By faith are you saved through Christ Jesus." That is true. No amount of bead telling, repetition of monotonous prayer, shrine visitation can ever catch up with our personal delinquencies. It is not a question of bringing sacrifices to an altar of an exacting deity. It is a question of attitude, the disposition of the heart. Repentance involves faith in God as revealed in Christ.

Trust is antecedent to assurance. God was in Christ, and faith is in effect belief in the revelation of God as seen in Christ. We must be born again. We become new men in Christ Jesus. The new man does not focus his thought upon his sin and ascertain how much payment with interest must be deposited in the heavenly bank to meet his obligation. Quite the contrary, he knows that confession and repentance are pleasing to a forgiving God, but they are not enough; there must be commitment. The mind must be centered upon the great positives of the Christian life. Christianity is not a body of negatives composed of "thou shalt nots"; it is made up of "thou shalts," the positives: "Thou shalt love the Lord thy God with all thy mind and heart and soul and thy neighbor as thyself"; "Thou shalt bear one another's burdens"; "Thou shalt be great as thou dost serve"; "A new commandment give I unto you, that you love one another as I have loved you." Life following repentance must reveal itself in a love that justifies forgiveness. Ascetics who fast perhaps think more about the food they do not eat than do men and women who are temperate and eat. Jesus came eating and drinking.

It may be thought that all of this is too easy. I think not. Repentance is not an easy matter. It is not the glib announcement, "The past is past, forget it." Sin cannot be forgiven quite so easily. The sin must be seen for what it is, a violation of God's will, an affront to the personality hurt by sin. It must be seen in all its stark hideousness. It must not be buried deep in consciousness to rise someday to haunt us. It must be exposed to the light. That is why confession is called for. Whether it be Mary Magdalene kneeling at the feet of Jesus, or Zaccheus coveting the presence of Christ in his home, or

Judas addressed by Jesus as friend at the very moment of betrayal, or a rich young ruler whose love of possessions kept him from full commitment to the Christian way — no matter what the sin — blasphemy, falsehood, lust, thievery, even murder (and men kill in different fashions, some in the heat of passion and some in the slow strangulation of a child's life as in the child-labor exploitation of yesterday) — the sin must be faced, and a brokenhearted penitent must confess it all. We used to sing, "Just as I am, without one plea." The sinner seeking salvation confessed and believed there was "welcome, pardon," that God would "cleanse, relieve." We sang the last verse: "Just as I am! Thy love unknown hath broken every barrier down; now, to be Thine, yea, Thine alone, O Lamb of God, I come!" The coming was based on faith — faith in God, faith in a promise, faith in love unfailing — but it involves more; the forgiven must become "Thine alone." Commitment is required. Here is an act of psychological cleansing based upon calm facing of sin. It is grounded in the certainty of love that will not let us go. The revolting nature of our acts must not be hidden by denials of unreality. The acts were real. So, too, is the love of God. That love constrains us.

There dawns upon the repentant a realization of how much he owes. We are debtors. My rights were won by men and women who died for free speech, freedom of assemblage, free press. These men and women won the right to insist that government derive its just powers by consent of the governed. Their sacrifices established the principle that man is endowed by his Creator with certain inalienable rights. The treasures in the realm of truth, goodness, and beauty are mine. I owe much. My debt climaxes in Christ's revelation of God. This is a gift indeed. Who can pay for such blessings? There is but one answer; Paul put it down: "Lead lives of love. . . . Copy God then as His beloved children. . . . Faith, hope, and love last on, these three; but the greatest of all is love."

It does seem a bit too easy. We must assume accountability for wrongdoing. Without God's grace, His active love, there could be no forgiveness. But assuming that love — or, to put it positively, in the light of that love — what does His justice demand? There is much suffering that flows from sin. It cannot be avoided, no matter how complete the forgiveness. There is restitution to be made, burdens to be borne. All of that is in the here and the now. My relationship to God is that of a son who has failed his Father but who comes at last to such understanding of his Father that he throws himself without recourse upon his Father's love. I cannot believe that an abstraction that posits humanity as responsible for Adam's sin is a fact. It is a fallacy conjured up by logicians to make a theory plausible. It simply will not do for a thinker to explain evil and suffering due to natural causes as flowing from a so-called original sin. Job was troubled by the question, "Why do the righteous suffer?" The good suffer with the evil. Sin has social consequences and war curses millions, good and bad alike. I simply do not have an answer. Perhaps the problem of evil will be solved satisfactorily someday. For me, I have never read an explanation that satisfies. From Augustine to Royce, read the answers, and pause to consider Edgar Sheffield Brightman's thesis. Dr. Brightman held that there were certain limitations to the power of God, that these limitations were not outside of God but within, namely, a factor in the divine nature itself that resists or frustrates the divine will, thereby preventing the world from being wholly free from suffering. This was an attempt on Dr. Brightman's part to face the fact that there is much suffering in nature that could not have been deliberately planned by a God who is good and righteous. He sought to explain this contradiction by insisting upon a factor within the divine nature itself that limits, or at least occasions struggle upon the part of God. A study of these explanations does not satisfy. After it all, I return to Job, and say, "Though He slay me, still will I trust Him." In Him there is plenteous mercy. Of that I am sure. In childlike trust I hold that nothing can separate me from the love of God and that this God was in Christ reconciling the world unto Himself. Thus I come to the moment of repentance in faith; I believe I am forgiven by a loving God, that I am summoned to live in the Way, the Truth, and the Life of Christ, and in so doing I meet the demands of justice. I must suffer for some of my acts where physical and moral laws have been broken. God is satisfied by my change of heart. I am a new man.

God Himself has taken the initiative in this matter of reconciliation. He does not wait for the prodigal to come to himself and return from the far country. God

has sought out the prodigal. The far countries are in-
habited by all of us. Many there are who do not know
that the Father seeks the lost son. God does not sit
upon a forbidding throne awaiting propitiatory gifts
from a son who has thrown his heritage away. No, the
Father has new raiment, a ring, and music awaiting the
son's return. This is the nature of the One who forgives.
The human cry, "God be merciful to me a sinner," is answered at once by a God of mercy whose Son declared,
"Blessed are the merciful: for they shall obtain mercy."
And for those who stand in defiance, daring to shake a
fist in the face of the Eternal, God continues to love, but
refuses to break the will of the one to whom He has
given freedom. He must await as a human father awaits
the return of a wayward son.

There is a problem here. I know it and I know that I
have not found an answer that will satisfy the legalist.
The power to sin inheres in the freedom with which God
endowed us. I am responsible for my action within that
freedom. Sin does separate me from God but never separates me from His love; sin keeps the love outside. "I
stand at the door and knock," said Jesus. We must open
the door. The Visitor is standing there. How can we
think of God standing forever at the door of our hearts,
eager to enter but awaiting our decision, and at the same
time think of God as One who is not mocked? He
stands there in the certainty of victory. Sooner or later
the sinning soul capitulates. Man may seek to subvert
the purpose of God, but in so doing struggles against the
nature of things. God does not stand afar off, a tran-

scendent Being satisfied to let His children, mothlike, fly to the flame. A God of love walks the second mile and the hundredth mile. He intervenes in history by so entering the life of Christ that He Himself suffers. Love is personified. Love does not fail. There is balm in Gilead. There is a spiritual therapy that makes us whole. "We know that in everything God works for good with those who love him, who are called according to His purpose." This is to affirm that God is at work in history, that just as the Creator, contemplating creation, saw that "it was good," so too the Sustainer, contemplating history, will someday look back upon it all and say, "It was good." He will look forward to all that may come, recognizing that man will still exercise his freedom and that some will still alienate themselves from God, but knowing that ultimately everything works for good — but with the qualification, to those who love Him. It is possible to say no indefinitely to God, but I, perhaps naïvely, continue to hold that God is eventually to be victor over every rebellious will and that the victory will be won not by coercion but by the unconquerable and transforming power of love.

In the Eighth Chapter of Romans Paul writes, in the certainty that means victory, "We know that in everything God works for good with those who love Him, who are called according to His purpose. . . . What then shall we say to this? If God is for us, who is against us? . . . Who shall separate us from the love of Christ? Shall tribulation, or distress, or persecution, or famine, or nakedness, or peril, or sword? . . . No, in all these things we are more than conquerors through Him who loved us. For I am sure that neither death, nor life, nor angels, nor principalities, nor things present, nor things to come, nor powers, nor height, nor depth, nor anything else in all creation, will be able to separate us from the love of God in Christ Jesus our Lord."

CHAPTER VII

I Believe in Man

IS MAN a god or a beast? Answers run the gamut from divinity to nature "red in tooth and claw." Some see man as Godlike, endowed with reason, possessing an unconquerable soul, a being destined to rule and to serve. Others see man as an animal, controlled by passion, self-seeking and ruthless, fighting in a struggle in which the fit survive. I have met men who were cruel and cunning. I have known men whose love, thought, and service were a benediction. Sometimes we think of humanity as marching irresistibly toward the promised land. Progress appears to be normal and inevitable, and utopia assured. Then we are brought up with a sickening start as we stand before the crematories of a Hitler regime, and mankind appears determined to return to the caves from which it emerged. Which is it: "To the strong belong the spoils" or "The meek shall inherit the earth"?

For myself, I must start with the fact that God created

us in His own image. He believed His work was good. True enough, man in his God-given freedom has at times alienated himself from God, at least we are so informed by the theologians. I find it difficult to think of man as abstraction. I have never met "man" in the collective sense. I have met individuals. True, we are enough alike to justify the generic term; nevertheless, it is the individual with whom I must deal. I think of man as a son of God and of God as the Father of us all. I am aware of the insistence in some quarters that this is a false assumption. There are those who argue arrogantly that no man is the son of God until he has accepted Christ and declared adherence to a man-made creed alleged to be final and therefore not subject to change. They speak of adoption. To me, this is to betray the very Christ they demand that we accept. If God is Father, we belong to one human family and are brothers. Man is endowed with regal dignity. No matter what the color of his skin, the place of his birth, or the faith in which he is reared, he is my brother.

I believe in man because of the capacities with which he is endowed. There is no limit to the outreaches of his intellect. *The Iliad* and *The Odyssey* were written by a man; so, too, *The Divine Comedy,* the plays of Shakespeare, and *Faust.* Dedicated men and women, disciplined and devout, have stood before chemistry tables and the physicist's desk — mathematicians, biologists, astronomers in observatories — all have driven themselves day and night in quest for truth. Alfred Noyes tells the story in *Torch Bearers.*

I have crossed the seas in heavier-than-air planes; I have entered disease-infested areas, protected by inoculation. I think of Louis Pasteur and all the men of medicine — "map-making" men who beat back the forces of disease and marched forward in the calm certainty that tomorrow sickness would be no more. I have talked to David Lilienthal, and I think not only of the Tennessee Valley Authority and of the Atomic Energy Commission, both of which he chaired, but now of the Development and Resources Company he heads. With engineers, he turns his genius toward Iran, and tomorrow controlled rivers will irrigate the desert lands, roses will bloom, and electric power will lift burdens from the backs of men and women and little children.

I believe the mind of man will shortly find answer to the problems of travel among the planets. New sources of power are sufficient answer to yesterday's fear that oil and coal reserves would soon be exhausted. In a word, I believe in man. His intellect is sufficient for the solution of his problems, for the phrasing of his thought and the pushing out to the answer to the last question. He is unconquerable, save only as he defies the moral law and destroys himself. This he can do. I do not believe he will.

He has infinite capacity for love. He can hate, too, but I believe in him because I have looked into the eyes of a mother holding a baby in her arms and into the eyes of a father whose son was receiving his degree at college. Men and women have given their lives for others and have revealed the "greater love" Jesus described. They have given their lives not only on the battlefield but in the laboratory and in the home. Four chaplains gave their life preservers to their comrades and went down together unafraid. Lazear is bitten by the mosquito and dies; and yellow fever dies too. In the old days we sang, "When the roll is called up yonder." If there be a calling of the roll of history, we shall hear the names of numberless men and women who gave their lives for truth, for beauty, for country, and for the world — scientists, writers of poetry and prose, explorers, men of government, teachers, and ministers of religion, heroes who endured unreasoning criticism, the gibbet, the pyre, chains and cell, hatred and scorn, but carried on and demonstrated that "love never disappears." Yes, but millions more unknown to history whose love lived in the home, the community, the nation — parents with their children, teachers with their students, missionaries in lands far from home — all these stand as witnesses to the infinite capacity of man to love. And in this "love divine, all loves excelling," the love that Jesus Himself revealed, we behold love that is at once the glory and the nature of God. Humanity itself is capable of such love. The lives of countless thousands bear testimony to that fact. Stephen, the first Christian martyr, was a man like you and me. The stones were falling and death was imminent, but he, like his Lord, prayed, "Father, lay not this sin up to their charge." I believe in man, a being who can love those who despitefully use him.

When God sought to break through the last barrier, He revealed Himself in a Person. The thunders of Sinai and the still, small voice were not enough. Christ was born of a woman and laid in a manger. God thought man of such worth that He chose man for His own incarnation. This is the supreme exaltation of man.

Christians of recent centuries have been so concerned to prove the deity of Jesus that they have well-nigh forgotten His humanity. It was His humanity the Apostles' Creed sought to make clear. He was born. He suffered. He was crucified. He died. He was buried. When we discuss the Trinity, we all too often forget that Jesus was once a child. The attributes of God were possessed by Jesus, it is said. It is recorded in the Book that Jesus grew in wisdom and in stature and in favor with God and man. Obviously, He could not be omniscient and at the same time grow in wisdom as a boy grows. God, as we have seen, took upon Himself the limitations of humanity when He chose to make Himself fully known to man. Jesus hungered, it is written. At times He was sorely troubled, His heart was heavy, He was weary and had no place to lay His head. God was in Christ, yes; and in Christ there is a full, perfect, and sufficient revelation of all that God is. But we must remember that Jesus was tempted. When in the home of His friend Lazarus, Jesus wept. He was a man in whom God made Himself fully known, so perfectly known, in fact, that we speak of the "God-man." Today, when we declare, "God is love," we understand its meaning because we have seen that love in Christ. I believe in man because God believes in man. He believed in him so much that He saw in man a fit habitation for Himself.

I believe in man because he has demonstrated that he, a lone individual, can stand against the massed power of class, race, or nation. He can refuse to bow to Baal. In the Spanish Revolution, a man declared that he would rather die upon his feet than live upon his knees. In *Key Largo*, Maxwell Anderson takes us into the disillusioned minds of young Americans who had enlisted in the forces of the Spanish Revolution. They were idealists, and possessed the courage idealism so often evokes; but a realistic facing of sinister forces present in the war had led to desperate decision. Anderson describes the scene. It is in northern Spain. Bright moonlight comes down across a rocky hilltop, revealing four young men on outpost guard duty. They are Americans dressed haphazardly in nondescript uniforms. King, their leader, says bitterly:

> Our cause is lost, that's all.
> Maybe because there isn't any God
> and nobody cares who wins. Anyway if you win
> you never get what you fight for, never get
> the least approximation of the thing
> you were sold on when you enlisted. No, you find
> instead that you were fighting to impose
> some monstrous, bloody injustice, some revenge
> that would end in another war.

He tells them that as students they had seen Spain as a bugle call. He speaks of Byron, who went to Greece a hundred years ago and died in a swamp of the fever, and of Don Quixote tilting at windmills. He says:

I know I'm a turncoat . . .
maybe I thought I talked like Rupert Brooke —
for all I know maybe I thought I looked
like that poor Galahad of Gallipoli,
saving heaven for the angels.

Victor, another of the young men, has lost faith in
God. He insists that "the sky's quite empty," but argues:

I have to believe
there's something in the world that isn't evil —
I have to believe there's something in the world
that would rather die than accept injustice — some-
    thing
positive for good — that can't be killed —
or I'll die inside.

King breaks in:

I tell you it was a dream,
all a dream we had, in a dream world,
of brothers who put out a helping hand
to brothers, and might save them. — Long ago
men found out the sky was empty; it follows
that men are a silly accident, meaningless,
here in the empty sky, like a flag on the moon,
as meaningless as an expedition led
to take possession of it — in the name of Marx —
or maybe democracy — or social justice!
Why should we die here for a dead cause, for a
    symbol,
on these empty ramparts, where there's nothing to
    win,
even if you could win it?

Victor replies — and here we behold the unbeatable man:

> Yes, but if I die
> then I know men will never give in;
> then I'll know there's something in the race
> of men, because even I had it, that hates injustice
> more than it wants to live. — Because even I had it —
> and I'm no hero. — And that means the Hitlers
> and the Mussolinis always lose in the end —
> force loses in the long run, and the spirit wins,
> whatever spirit is. Anyway it's the thing
> that says it's better to sit here with the moon
> and hold them off while I can. If I went with you
> I'd never know whether the race was turning
> down again, to the disosaurs — this way
> I keep my faith. In myself and what men are.
> And in what we may be.

I believe in man. He can stand at times disillusioned and in despair, faith gone and fearful of empty sky, but, nonetheless, with head unbowed. This is the being who, with faith restored, alerted and committed, will overcome the world.

Jesus suffered a cross, and transformed it into a symbol of salvation. He loved and forgave His tormentors, and died with a prayer upon His lips. Others have done so too. They have faced the firing squad without hate. I do not mean that all men live upon such an exalted plane, but the fact that men have done so validates my belief that man possesses such capacity. I know that battlefields have become slaughterhouses and that war is a bout of butchery. I know the prisoners of Hitler were bled to death to secure blood plasma for soldiers.

I shall never forget the room. It was perhaps sixteen by twenty, with rough flooring and unplastered walls. It was at Buchenwald. Here the "doctors" examined prisoners. Here experiments were performed. German doctors, German prisoners — all of the New Order. It was the day after our forces had taken Weimar when I visited the concentration camp. A prisoner, now liberated, stood at the doorway and said, "I don't know what happened in this room, but I saw from twenty to forty enter every day. At the close of the day I saw the piles of bodies taken away from that room over there." He pointed to an adjoining room. "They tried out serums. They tested reactions to pain, to heat, to cold." Men used other men as guinea pigs. So low does man sink. There are those who say, "How can you believe in man?" I know, he can become a devil. I can understand those who see man as fallen, cursed by original sin, alienated from God, a beast. Man can be all of this. He can torture his fellows with a diabolical cruelty unknown to the jungle. He can become a sadist too revolting to describe. This I know; but he can also carry a Cross to Calvary; he can die for a friend; he can be merciful; he can love. The Terrible Meek conquers the terror of Rome.

I believe in man because he is a rational being. He cannot fulfill his destiny except as he exercises reason. Given freedom within which to reason, man transcends his limitations. He soon learns there is only so much food that can be eaten, so much raiment that can be worn. He tires of the palace and turns to the cottage. Overindulgence in sex becomes impotency. The physical has its limitations. But in the realm of the intellect and in the life of the spirit, the road leads upward to the light. The mind moves on. It enters new worlds that are but gateways to more new worlds, and thus it goes.

James Matthew Barrie in the meaningful dialogue of *Dear Brutus* has a character ask, "We have the power to shape ourselves?" And the answer is given, "We have the power right enough." They have been discussing Shakespeare's "The fault, dear Brutus, is not in our stars but in ourselves, that we are underlings." Man possesses God-given reason. It is a gift never to be discounted. In it lies the power to realize dreams. It is when man thinks things are impossible that he despairs. William Faulkner has said, "I believe that man will not only endure; he will prevail. He is immortal, not because he alone among creatures has an inexhaustible voice but because he has a soul, a spirit capable of compassion and sacrifice and endurance. The poet's, the writer's, duty is to write about these things. It is his privilege to help man endure by lifting his heart, by reminding him of the courage and honor and hope and pride and conscience and pity and sacrifice which have been the glory of the past." Yes, we must lift up our hearts. When the minister repeats the words, "Lift up your hearts," that bit of service is called the "Sursum Corda." It is a world-wide Sursum Corda that is called for today.

It is the linkage of reason and of love that assures victory. Albert Schweitzer has considered the rational animal at work. He knows and we all know that the term "animal" is not pleasing. Man, no doubt, is an animal, but he is also soul and mind. He worships. He thinks. He loves. Emancipation awaits the union of thought and of love. Schweitzer writes, "The essential element in Christianity as it was preached by Jesus and as it is comprehended by thought is this, that it is only through love that we can attain to communion with God. All living knowledge of God rests upon this foundation: that we experience Him in our lives as Will-to-love."

It is not to worship ourselves to appreciate and to appraise our capacities. Man has been able to move out beyond his selfish interests, beyond his family, his tribe and clan, beyond the nation, beyond his race. The Hebrew prophets preached universality. The righteousness of God, the love of God involve the universe. Man now enters a new world, a world in which all humanity lives, a world in which we are to be educated for universal living. Radhakrishnan concludes his thoughtful and inspiring volume *East and West, the End of Their Separation* with these words: "We are living at the dawn of a new era of universal humanity. . . . Whether we like it or not, we live in one world and require to be educated to a common conception of human purpose and destiny. . . . We will unite the peoples of all races in a *community, catholic, comprehensive* and *co-operative.* The history of the new world, the one world, has begun."

I rebel against contemporary endeavors to discount man. When man turns to religion on the one hand and science on the other, he can, with the reason with which God has endowed him, abolish war and establish peace, fashion economic justice, and set up racial brotherhood. It is an affront to God, at least so it seems to me, when we make light of the capacities with which he has endowed us. What did Jesus mean when He said, "Greater works shall ye do than I do"?

I hold this faith after having seen man and his baseness, his greed, his passions. For ten years I served a church on the east side of Los Angeles. The waves of life's storms beat against the shores of our service. Greedy men in the name of what they called "good business" took the old one-family cottages and remodeled them to house four families. The rent was quadrupled, and slum conditions developed behind the façade of cottage respectability. Each day of the years of service at the Church of All Nations brought its toll of human problems. We dealt with the people themselves. It was not like the class in sociology where we discussed situations that were described by an author. We dealt not with cases, but with persons. A woman ran away with a man. She left a bewildered husband and two little girls; he left a self-possessed wife with a young daughter and a younger son. The deserted husband's first request to Mrs. Oxnam was for her to accompany the little girls to a store to buy new dresses and new hats for Easter — "I don't know where to go or what they should wear." The woman who had been deserted lived courageously, and saw her son and daughter through the university. Her husband was declared legally dead. I wonder where he is today. Or again, I called at another home. Officers were in front of and behind the house. The wife had telephoned, "Please come." Her husband was in bed, broken nervously. He had embezzled more than fifty thousand dollars. I was at the station when they took him away to San Quentin. Or again, a boy who had been given narcotics and had become an addict stole, shot an officer, and was hanged. He was eighteen. Just before they took him away, he said, "I wouldn't treat a dog like this." Yes, I have seen life at low levels. I have seen battlefields where we killed and were killed, and I have seen the gas chambers at Dachau. I have read the testimony of men who hired themselves out as professional witnesses and perjured others into prison. I have met respectable citizens, churchgoers, holding offices of importance, who were willing to manipulate the elected representatives of the people in such fashion as to secure special privilege that sometimes meant millions of dollars.

I can understand the pessimism of some religious thinkers whose only answer is, "Man is a fallen creature, cursed by original sin, disposed to evil, damned unless he accepts Christ." But this is not man as I see him. I see man as God's own handiwork. Man was created by God. I see him endowed with reason, a being of infinite capacities. I am constantly aware of the love that is ever present in the homes of the world, the love of a man for his wife, or the love of children for parents and parents for children. I know there is a fundamental contradiction in society. On Sunday we declare, "He who would be the greatest among you must become the servant of all," and too often during the weekday we insist, "Self-interest is the only sufficient motive to drive men to real achievement." But I know what men and women can be. I see man as fit for the incarnation of God; and in Jesus I see what he can become. I believe in man.

I realize that in what I have said there is contradiction. I have suggested that truth can be apprehended by intuition. I have also said I am pledged to the scientific attitude of mind. I know that thinking is required to reach truth. I would not rush into the company of the mystics. I know that the Apostle Paul told us that at present we see through a glass darkly. It may be an admission that at this very place I grope. I do. I do not know how to define my terms. We use the word "spiritual" and stand confused before a realm that has been penetrated by but a few. We are told to worship God in spirit and in truth. I think each one of us knows that he is related to other men and women and that this relationship is more than is found in the ties of blood or citizenship or church. It is a spiritual relationship. He knows that beyond the drives that are apparently essential for the perpetuation of the race and beyond the tendency to place the self in the center of the universe, there is something more; sometimes we call it the real self. It is the self that is given to truth, goodness, and beauty, the self that thinks of others, the self that finds itself in love. Or, to put it another way, it is the self that is realized in the complete gift of self to others. It is the self requisite to the practice of brotherhood. Paul tells us that knowledge will be superseded. "Faith, hope, and love last on, these three, but the greatest of all is love." Am I merely engaged here in the reassembling of words? Perhaps so. I believe that man can master the mysteries of his own inner life. I think we are at that task.

If God were but an image made of precious metal, it would be possible to measure, weigh, analyze, and come at last to a scientific report on the nature of God. But God is not a graven image. All that I have said is based upon a fundamental assumption, namely, that God exists, and this means for me that He is at least as much as personality. He is a living Being. He is a Spirit. Man, too, is a spirit. Have we sought to explore the spirit by the use of instruments capable of measuring all else but the spirit? At the moment of writing, the scientists of the world, in a cooperative endeavor that knows neither iron curtain nor bamboo barrier, are searching for all the facts that have to do with the earth. We speak of the International Geophysical Year. Out of this cooperation will come new correlations and greater comprehension. A similar search in the realm of the spirit may lead to life more abundant than man has known. I believe in man because I am sure that all his achievements to the present are but the first steps of a journey that leads from the plains to the plateaus and that beyond are the mountain ranges and the sunrises.

I believe in man because I see in him not only a member of my family, my community, my nation, but a person created by God, an individual of intrinsic worth. He has this worth whether he be Chinese, Russian, or British; whether he be black, brown, white, yellow, or red;

whether he be Buddhist, Hindu, or Christian. I have said elsewhere and have often reiterated that men and not things are the goal of social living. We speak of the supremacy of personality and the infinite worth of persons. "Reverence for life" is Schweitzer's phrase.

Acknowledged or repudiated, men whose philosophies are as separated as the distance between the poles appear to be moved by this recognition of or feeling for the worth of man. How do we account for the blazing indignation of the revolutionist, the moral denunciations of the prophet, the sorrowing heart of Jesus as He looked upon the great city and cried, "O Jerusalem, Jerusalem"? Surely it is not because of the exploitation the revolutionist confronts, the moral law the prophet has apprehended, or the rejection of the good Jesus beheld. It must be more. It must be that man is seen for what he is — a brother, a son of God.

Eliseo Vivas in *The Moral Life and the Ethical Life* declares, "The intrinsic value of the person is constituted by the value he possesses as spirit." Vivas has difficulty in defining spirit. Apparently all men do. I agree with him when he says, "To repudiate these speculations, however, because they do not have the clarity and distinctness that we find in mathematical analysis or in the positive sciences, is possible only to positivists, to whom subject matter is of no intrinsic importance and only the way in which it has been manipulated counts. But to deny that they are inconclusive is unworthy of a student of philosophy. To this writer, at any rate, it is the subject matter which is of chief importance, and if vagueness

and obscurity are all that he can achieve, he sees in such
inadequate results a reason, not for abandoning the
problem, but for doing his best with it."

It may be that the search for answer in the realm of the
spirit will end at the place Augustine reached long ago
when he prayed, "Thou has made us for Thyself, and our
hearts are restless until they find rest in Thee."

I believe in democracy because I believe in man. Carl
Sandburg sings of "The People, Yes." The people blun-
der. They are trapped. They are fooled. They can be
dressed up in black shirts and brown; they can march under swastika and hammer and sickle. They can be per-
suaded by raucous voice and propaganda page. They
vote the scoundrels in. But there comes a day of reckon-
ing. In the long run, the people, yes. Unless we can believe that, the democratic dream vanishes. The voice at
Gettysburg, a single voice, has become the voice of millions; and these millions will yet be heard in Hungary
and Poland, in satellite lands, and in the great center of
tyranny. Government of the people, by the people, for
the people will not perish, unless the people themselves
lose faith in man. There is something God-given in
man's scorn of tyranny. Neither torture nor brainwashing, propaganda nor police can destroy the inner resolve to be free. There is something in the constitution
of man that drives him to destroy the dictator. I believe
it was put there by the Creator. I believe in man. I think
he will preserve his freedom. I hold he will use that freedom to bring peace to warring humanity, justice to ex-
ploited humanity, brotherhood to segregated humanity.

Man is about to recognize his brother. He is learning that class, race, and nation are concepts too small to unite mankind to win world law and order and enduring peace. The so-called return to religion is in part the determination to find the larger unifying concept he needs. He seeks a faith, and many find it in the life and thought of a World Saviour whose ethic is love, not love for self and immediate family, not love for treasured culture and for nation, not for these alone, but universal love, within whose embrace is all humanity. We are ready for it, and it is ready for us. I believe man is capable of widening the range of his affection, and I believe he will.

I saw an American officer in Innsbruck lift an Austrian child into his arms and hold her close. We had been walking together, and the child had looked up into his face, smiled, and given him a flower. I said, "What about 'no fraternization'?" His face clouded. "I did not come over here to fight children," he said. It was in Korea that a veteran said, "The cries of the children got me." I believe man will abolish war, because war is more than jets and rockets, artillery, and hydrogen bombs. It is fire and hunger and hatred, debris and debauchery. It is the cry of a child. It has been a long time since Isaiah, and swords are not yet plowshares; spears are not pruning hooks. I know. Bombs are tested, and scientists discuss "fall-out."

Whittaker Chambers, former conspirator and more recently chief witness in the Hiss case, seems to have lost faith in man. He writes, "It is idle to talk about preventing the wreck of Western civilization. It is already a wreck from within. That is why we can hope to do little more now than to snatch a fingernail of a saint from the rack or a handful of ashes from the faggots, and bury them secretly in a flower pot against the day, ages hence, when a few men begin again to dare to believe that there was once something else, that something else is thinkable, and need some evidence of what it was and the fortifying knowledge that there were those who, at the great nightfall, took loving thought to preserve the tokens of hope and truth."

What happens to great minds like Spengler, who concludes, "By a thousand signs, this is the century of fascism," or lesser brains like Chambers, who would "snatch a fingernail of a saint from the rack or a handful of ashes from the faggots"? Mussolini was hung up by his feet in Milan, and Hitler sent a bullet crashing into his morbid brain. Is this the century of fascism? Stalin lies in the Red Square mausoleum, and hard by Khrushchev accuses and condemns him. For Chambers, Western civilization is a wreck, and his mind looks down the years to a day when man will think of "something else," but for the present, it is the "great nightfall." How dare such a voice speak of "tokens of hope and truth"!

The truth is here. Hope is present. "Something else" is thinkable now. I believe in man. I hold he will find peace of mind and peace of soul, not in the neat Coué formulas of some clergymen, but in the Cross of Christ. It towers o'er the wrecks of time. It is symbol and summons. There is a Father of us all. His love is unfailing. It is love amazing and divine. It is the Way. I believe that Christ lifted up will draw all men to Him. These new men in Christ Jesus, these men with the mind that was in Christ, will, I believe, abolish war and give us peace, abolish exploitation and give us justice, abolish discrimination and give us fellowship. Naïve? The stuff of which dreams are made? Perhaps.

I speak of Jesus Christ as Saviour. I believe man can be saved from his sins. This is a negative way of putting it. I believe man can be summoned to move out in terms of truth, goodness, beauty. He is called to love God and brother. "If ye love Me, ye will keep My commandments," said Jesus. I believe man can both love Christ and keep His commandments. I believe he will. He needs power. He cannot do this alone. The power is available. "Ye shall receive power," Jesus declared. Man is capable of absolute commitment to Christ. In that commitment, power is found. This is a power that does not curtail freedom. It creates freedom. It is a power held in trust. It finds life by giving life.

I can hear certain comment. Is he unaware of the hyena in man? No, I have seen the hyena. In fact, I know the tiger is present. I know that sincere and studious men hold that beneath the thin skin of civilization is the red blood of the jungle beast. But I have also seen great souls. I know what man can do, what he can be. Gandhi lived in our own generation, and Schweitzer continues to heal broken bodies in black Africa and seeks through persuasion to heal disordered minds in white America. I have seen children at play — and great men at creative tasks. I believe in man.

I know that my Redeemer liveth. God is a living Being. Man has access to the divine. Jesus said, "I am the door." I believe that door is opened to every man who knocks. I see mankind passing through that door. We shall know as we are known. Mysteries will be penetrated. We shall learn that faith, hope, and love are the abiding forces, but the greatest of all is love.